AN INTRODUCTION TO

INN SIGNS

AN INTRODUCTION TO
INN SIGNS

ERIC R. DELDERFIELD

KING'S ARMS

David and Charles

Contents

Contents

List of Illustrations

Preface

THE history of the English inn and the wealth of tales about so many of them form such a well-nigh inexhaustible subject that I was happy to accede to my Publisher's request for another book to follow the two brief guides and one major volume resulting from my previous excursions into this field.

One writer has referred to inn signs as a great open-air portrait gallery which covers the British Isles. But the gallery includes far more than portraits. Every type of transport is pictured, from the coracles of the early Britons to coaches, trams, ships, motorcars, aeroplanes, flying-boats and even the more mundane bicycle. There are signboards depicting animals, birds, fish, insects and legendary beasts, as well as kings and queens, dukes and lords, statesmen, soldiers, sailors, airmen, poachers, fat men and giants.

We should be grateful too, that so much of history, geography, legend and fairy tale is kept alive by the name or sign of the 'local'. As history is being made, so the brewery companies and individual licensees are quick to record it by new signs. Typical examples are *Sir Francis Chichester*, Plymouth (Devon), *Flying Saucer*, Gillingham (Kent), and *Man in Space*, Stoke on Trent (Staffs). Even a popular television programme is represented with its name and sign—*Dock Green*.

No other country in the world has a counterpart to the British inn with its centuries-old traditions and few other institutions can have served our race more diligently in such a variety of ways. Inns have been coroners' courts, courtrooms for quarter sessions, smugglers' headquarters, centres for friendly societies and it was an inn that gave birth to the music hall. Recently in Devon, a room in an inn was turned into a temporary church. The Pharmaceutical Society was founded in a tavern, and the American national anthem was first played in a London inn. Above all, inns have been a 'village club' to generations of countrymen.

By choice as well as for convenience, the word 'inn' has been used throughout this book. I feel it is more 'snug' than 'hotel' or 'tavern' and, however grandiose the name we may give to their successors, they all sprang from the humble English inn.

Though, happily, good inn signs flourish and continue to multiply, not all brewery companies are yet fully alive to the value of individual signs; they have still to learn, it seems, that while few will stop because some particular brand of ale is advertised, there is ample evidence of people halting to explore when a witty, attractive, informative or intriguing sign is sighted.

Today there are some 70,000 inns in the British Isles and with the increasing interest now being shown on the part of both the public and the brewery trade it is to be hoped that each will one day have its own attractive signboard to add colour and interest to our roads.

Exmouth   E. R. DELDERFIELD
1969

PART ONE

From the Beginning

THE earliest inns or taverns came into being when tracks first became roads and, ever since, it has been their custom to display a sign to notify the traveller that there refreshment could be obtained. One of the earliest recognised signs of an ale house or wine shop was a display of vine leaves or a bush, always associated with Bacchus, god of wine, and there is little doubt that this sign was brought to Britain by the Romans and its usage generally adopted.

When the two Roman cities of Pompeii and Herculaneum were excavated from the deluge of lava and ash that had engulfed them for hundreds of years, it became apparent that most of their shops had displayed a sign outside. In the ruins of Herculaneum alone there were no less than 900 signboards of drinking houses and other trades. A schoolmaster exhibited a plaque showing a man thrashing a boy. The goat was the sign of a dairy. Most numerous was the sign of the 'Chequers', believed to have indicated a drinking house where a game of draughts could be played on the premises, and the existence of several hundred *Chequers* in this country today may be another legacy from the Roman Conquest, though it could also be accounted for by the fact that it was, in medieval times, the sign of the money-changer, which perhaps explains why there are a number of inns of this name in seaports.

While the *Vine* was certainly the earliest type of inn sign, others soon followed as travelling increased and it became necessary to distinguish between rival houses in the same street or vicinity. Each landlord then erected his own sign bearing a distinctive name or symbol by which his customers would know him and which would serve as an address.

At first, the illiteracy of the common people doubtless contributed in no small measure to the need for such signs but they continued to proliferate and by the time many more people could read, and travelling had become widespread, inn signs were already firmly established as a colourful and traditional English custom.

From the reign of Richard II in the fourteenth century publicans were singled out from other trades and compelled, by law, to exhibit a sign. A new brew had to be tasted and receive official approval before it could be offered for sale. Special officials, chosen annually by the civic authorities, were assigned to this task and failure to observe the letter of the law in testing the quality of the brew could result in a punishment as severe as a ducking in the river.

By the end of the fourteenth century competition between inns had become so fierce that merely to show a recognised emblem was not enough, and publicans began to vie with one another in displaying bigger and better signs of their calling. So successful was the trade and so unquenchable the thirst of the customer that new problems began to arise, and by the sixteenth century the authorities were making some effort to limit the number of taverns. Only forty were licensed in the entire City of London and other towns and cities were allotted a quota. Even so, when the population of England and Wales totalled only five million, there were 13,000 licensed premises to serve them and this at a time when ale was three pints a penny. By 1656, the number of ale-house keepers in London had risen to well over 1,000.

In the fifteenth century the headquarters of the brewery trade were in Love Lane, in the City of London, a street which derived its name from the activities of certain professional ladies. On one occasion at least, this organisation was convicted and fined £20 for selling dear ale and the masters were imprisoned until the fine was paid. It is of special interest to note that the charge was laid by Dick Whittington.

Many of the old City alehouses had their signs carved in stone on the outside of the house, as had been the custom at Pompeii in Roman times, and in the rebuilding which followed the Fire of London many of these slab-type signs were recovered and placed in the Guildhall Museum, where they may still be seen. They include the *Goose & Gridiron*, *Three Crowns*, *Three Kings*, *Three Bells*, *Ape & Apple* and *George & Dragon*. Another, the *Bull's Head*, was made from a sheet of iron. The *Cock & Bottle* was of later date, and is made of tiles similar to the splendid modern sign of the *Three Cranes* in the city of York.

A carved hardwood swing sign followed the plaque type and finally, in an effort to attract still more attention, a massive structure spanning the full width of the road became the vogue for those who could afford it. A few of each type are still to be found, but the swinging board is today by far the most popular.

More laws affecting innkeepers were enacted through the centuries, including one which restricted the size and weight of the so-called 'gallows' or 'beam' signs. Money was lavished upon these and one elaborate example erected at the *White Hart*, Scole (Norfolk) towards the end of the seventeenth century included some twenty-five life-size figures in its design and cost £1,000. Early in the eighteenth century one of these huge signs in London dragged down the front of the house to which it was attached and two people were killed as it crashed into the street. Nevertheless, in spite of public concern, it was not until 1797 that a law was passed ordering the dismantling of all such signs which could be reasonably held to be a danger, encroachment or annoyance to the general public.

There are today very few of these 'gallows' signs left, although most which do remain are excellent examples. One such is at the *Fox & Hounds*, Barley (Herts). The cross-bar extends across the road and carved on it in silhouette is a fox with the hounds and huntsmen in full cry. It commemorates a famous run when the hard-pressed fox was eventually run to earth in the yard of the inn.

Other 'beam'-type signs include the *Magpie*, Stoneham (Suffolk), *Four Swans*, Waltham Cross (Herts), the *Swan*, Stroud (Glos), the much photographed *Ye Olde Starre*, York and the *Green Man & Black's Head*, Ashbourne (Derbys).

The Pilgrim Hostels

IN the great wave of religious fervour which swept the fourteenth century vast numbers of pilgrims visited shrines of saints and martyrs over a very wide area and something had to be done to accommodate them. Wealthy travellers were automatically guests of abbeys and monasteries but there was nowhere the ordinary pilgrim could obtain lodging and refreshment until the religious houses began to erect hospices or hostels, generally adjacent to their own buildings, in all the principal centres where there were important shrines. There are many inns along the Pilgrims Way which owe their foundation to this. At Westhumble (Surrey) the *Stepping Stones* is a reminder of the old pilgrim's route which there crossed the river Mole.

Each hostel had a sign associated in some way with the religious house responsible for it. The *Bull*, one of the most popular signs today, was in the first place derived from La Boule (Latin, *bulla*), the seal of a collegiate body or monastery. A number of similar hostels were built by the Knights of St John of Jerusalem. Still existing of these are the *White Horse*, Dorking (Surrey), the *Angel*, Grantham (Lincs) and many more.

When Thomas á Becket was murdered in Canterbury Cathedral and acclaimed a martyr, pilgrims came in their thousands from all parts of the country and even from abroad to see and pray by his relics, for it was believed that by so doing almost any disease could be cured. A special hostel was built at Glastonbury (Som) in the middle of the fifteenth century to accommodate these pilgrims and this inn, the *George & Pilgrim*, is still in existence as is the *George*, Norton St Philip (Som). At Hurley (Berks) is the *Olde Bell*, a venerable inn which was a guest house of the monastery in 1135 and still dispenses hospitality to travellers.

Many of these monastic hostels remain, and broadly speaking have served their original purpose of catering for the traveller ever since. One such is the famous galleried *New Inn*, Gloucester. Built in 1457, it stands close to the cathedral which contains the shrine of the martyred king, Edward II, and this magnificent edifice was, in fact, rebuilt from the enormous revenues derived from the pilgrim traffic. A few miles away at Winchcombe, also in Gloucestershire, is the *George Inn*, which served the abbeys of Winchcombe and Hailes, the latter providing a particularly good example of the attraction that holy relics held for the people in medieval times.

The monastic hostels brought into being many signs

derived from religion and a great number are still popular.
They include: *Star, Seven Stars, Angel, Ark, Mitre, Salutation, Anchor, Ship* (a reference to the Ark), *Cross Keys*
(a reference to St Peter), *Lion & Lamb, Samson & the Lion,*
Halesowen (Worcs), which is today probably the only one
of that name. The *Lamb & Flag* was originally a religious
sign, particularly associated with the Crusades. It then
represented the Holy Lamb and later became the crest of
the Merchant Tailors. The *Bell*, of which there are a great
many, also comes into this category as it was frequently
close to a cathedral—as at Gloucester, until it was demolished in latter years—or the parish church in a small town
like Ilminster (Som).

The Crusades, too, inspired many popular signs and in
this category still are: *Trip to Jerusalem*, Nottingham;
Jerusalem, London; *White Knight* (sometimes shown as a
chess piece); *Gentil Knyght*, and most numerous of all,
Turk's Head and *Saracen's Head*. A variation of the latter
is *Blackamoor's Head*.

After the Reformation, churchwardens were often
responsible for brewing beer and many parishes had their
brewhouses adjacent to the church. The ale was consumed
at what were called 'Ale Frolics', the main object being
to raise revenue for church funds, though they were also
held for other reasons. 'Bid Ales', sometimes called 'Help
Ales', were for raising money for a poor man but as these
occasions tended to develop into orgies they gradually fell
into disuse. There are, however, still a great many inns
at the very gates of village churches, particularly in the
West Country, and some still retain the title of *Church
House*. In the Exeter area alone, eight still bear the name.
Others similarly situated are of even older foundation,
the *Church House* inn, at Harberton (Devon), for example,
having originally been a twelfth-century chantry house for
monks.

Page 17: A typical English scene which may be found all over the country

Page 18: A first-class example of an heraldic inn sign, Burley, near Leeds

Coaching Days

FROM the days of the pilgrims, inns became firmly established and their next great advance came when, with the improvement of roads, the coaching era dawned. Haphazard attempts at founding some system of public transport had been made from the middle of the sixteenth century, but it was not until nearly 200 years later, when the turnpike trusts became fully effective, that regular services were established between principal towns.

In 1731, the journey from London to Gloucester by coach took three days, and that from London to York about a week. The conditions were so difficult that only the most hardy could accomplish the journeys and it was little wonder that all the handbills and timetables bore the proviso: 'If God permits'!

Halfway through the eighteenth century a 'flying coach' service was introduced which completed the journey between London and Manchester in four and a half days and from then on progress was rapid. Many attempts were made to interest the Government in carrying the mails in especially fast vehicles, but for a long time the Post Office remained unconvinced, prejudiced and obstinate. Nevertheless, with private enterprise forcing the pace, coach services steadily improved and this improvement was matched by that of the inns, some of which developed into large and flourishing undertakings.

As the timetables of the coaches became tighter so the service at the inns on the route had perforce to keep up with the pace that was set. Innkeeping became a highly efficient and intensely competitive business, and the organisation must often have been superb for some fast runs allowed only a minute in which to change horses.

B

When the mail coaches became established they used to load at various inns and then assemble at the Central Post Office in London before starting their journeys. The *Bull & Mouth*, St Martin's-le-Grand, became the centre of an enormous industry. By 1830, twenty-one coaches were leaving there daily on scheduled runs to the north-west of England. The *Swan with two Necks*, Gresham Street, was another loading point and the *Talbot*, Borough High Street, which stood on the site of Chaucer's *Tabard*, was also an important coaching centre, as was the *Black Lion*, near Whitefriars Street, on the site now occupied by Northcliffe House. The service at the *Old White Bear*, a great galleried inn by Piccadilly, achieved particular coaching fame.

The *Bull & Mouth*, originally the *Boulogne Mouth* in honour of Henry VIII's capture of Boulogne harbour, had a sign depicting a bull's face with a wide mouth and this the owner, Sherman, adopted as his symbol and had painted on the doors of his yellow and black coaches. He quickly established a successful business and his vehicles, which included the 'Shrewsbury Wonder' and the 'Manchester Telegraph', accomplished the London-Manchester journey of 186 miles in about seventeen hours. It was Sherman who built huge underground stables beneath his yard to accommodate some of the 700-odd horses he always had on hand.

Pictures which remain to us of these inns show them with huge yards and two or three tiers of galleries, which accommodated the bedrooms. They had great coffee rooms and the large number of travellers arriving every day and night (often right through the night) were served promptly and well.

William Chaplin was the largest coach and inn proprietor in London, and owned some 1,500 horses and more than sixty coaches. His income was said to have been something in the region of half-a-million pounds a year. By contrast, the smaller inns operated by taking a share in a coach and agreeing to provide horses, although this was quite an expensive business.

Once the success of carrying the Post Office mails by coach was established, the services were extended considerably and by the end of the eighteenth century were covering some 2½ million miles a year.

Posting inns in the great days of coaching all had a large mural clock in a japanned case, which came to be known as the coaching or inn clock. In 1797, when Parliament put a tax on private clocks, they became known as 'Parliament' clocks, though the type of clock had been in use for many years before. Whatever name we choose to accept, the clocks were quite distinctive, with large dials clearly lettered, and were intended to serve the same purpose as did the clocks at railway stations in later years.

The inns also organised the posting system, hiring out post-chaises and postboys on a mileage basis. The postboys accompanied the carriages and were usually attired in a bright-coloured livery and received their keep from the innkeepers who hired them out. For their income they depended on tips.

A great many inns still bear signs of the coaching era, as for instance the superb and informative *Glocester Flying Machine*, Brockleworth (Glos). A very fine piece of work, it recalls one of the first 'flying coach' services, which operated three times a week from Gloucester to London. It pictures six horses pulling the great cumbersome coach which—despite its more flattering name—was used on the run.

One of the crack West Country mail coaches was the 'Quicksilver Mail', known by name throughout the length of its run—a sure sign of popularity, for mail coaches, unlike those which were privately owned, did not officially possess names. A handsome sign perpetuates this coach service at an inn at East Coker, nr Yeovil (Som). The mails were carried from London to Devonport, and the London to Exeter stretch of 176 miles was accomplished in its heyday in seventeen hours, an average speed of 10¼ miles an hour and necessitating twenty changes of horses. Later the service was extended to Falmouth (Cornwall).

Many fine inns developed in the provincial towns between which regular services were maintained. The Oxford-Cheltenham coach, 'Blenheim', ran on Mondays, Wednesdays and Fridays via Eynsham, Witney and Northleach. Drawn by four horses, it left Oxford at 2.30, and arrived at Cheltenham at 7 p.m. The distance was 40¼ miles and the fare 7s 6d. The 'Defiant' was a daily Cheltenham-Cambridge coach on which the fare was 32s 6d.

The *Flying Bull* inn, Rake (Hants) takes its name from two famous coaches, the 'Fly' and the 'Bull', which served the London to Portsmouth route. Incidentally, the inn is unique in that the building is actually astride the Hampshire/Sussex border and rates are levied on the house by both county authorities. Also associated with the coaching era are inns still bearing such names as *Horse & Groom*, *Gate*, *Tollgate*, *Turnpike House*, *Chain & Gate* etc. Less well-authenticated but immortally associated with the days of stage-coaches is the notorious highwayman after whom the *Dick Turpin*, East Finchley, London, is named. Turpin is also said to have frequented the *Ram Jam*, Stretham (Rutland) and *Turpin's Cave*, Epping (Essex) but the *Crown*, Hampstead (Essex), according to a plaque on the wall, claims to have been his birthplace.

The goods wagons of the period also used the innkeepers as agents for picking up and dropping goods, though they generally tended to avoid inns favoured by the coach traffic. A colourful sign of the carriers remains at *Ye Olde*

Waggon, Belsay (Northumb), where an attractive picture of the vehicles used swings outside the inn. Many more reminders are still with us as, for instance, *Jolly Waggoner* and *Carter's Rest*, *Van & Horses*, Uxbridge (Middx), etc.

The coaching era lasted just 100 years and the advent of the railways had a disastrous effect on the turnpike trusts and the coaching fraternity generally. At Egham (Surrey), prior to the opening of the railways, there were between seventy and eighty long-distance stage-coaches passing through the town, many of which stopped so that travellers could be refreshed and the horses changed. As the railways expanded, this number dropped to four and everywhere inns began to close on a wholesale scale. At Ashbourne (Derbys) there were a number of posting houses, but most of them were driven out of business and only one sizable inn, the *Green Man & Black's Head*, remains today. The last regular London-based mail coach was that operating between London and Norwich, which was routed through Newmarket. Founded in 1785, it ended in 1846. In the more rural districts, of course, some coach services carried on to a much later date.

The first mail to be carried by rail was between Liverpool and Manchester in 1830 and by the 1840s trains were gradually usurping the function of coaches. Many inns on the old coaching routes throughout the country were forced to close, some fortunately placed succeeded in adapting themselves to the different requirements of rail travellers while others, including some of the smaller ones on the by-roads, managed to survive until the arrival of the motor-car brought them a new lease of life.

Inns by the Water

THE rivers were the highways of this country long before
the roads, and wherever watermen were likely to stop for
refreshment an inn soon came into being. London's river
Thames still has its quota, many of which have been in
business for hundreds of years. Among the famous, and
known all over the world, is the *Prospect of Whitby*, Wap-
ping, whose name dates back to the 1830s, though the inn
itself is much older. In those days one of the vessels bringing coal and stone from Yorkshire to London was the
'Prospect', a three-master from Whitby, which always
moored opposite the inn and in course of time became a
landmark and the name of the inn. Samuel Pepys was
among the many famous people who patronised the place
in its earlier days.

Across the river is the *Mayflower*, which changed its
name from the *Shippe* when the 'Mayflower' sailed for
the new world in 1620. Close by is the *Angel*, reputedly
once a smuggler's hideout. Farther up-river at Isleworth
is the *London Apprentice*, a dignified eighteenth-century
building and at Greenwich, deservedly so, is the *Trafalgar
Tavern*, where the rooms bear the names of famous
admirals including: Hood, Hardy, Rodney and Duncan.
At Lambeth there is the appropriately named *Old Father
Thames* and, at Chelsea, the *King's Head & Eight Bells*, a
name said to derive from the custom of ringing bells on the
river whenever Charles II was afloat. Interesting though the
story is, the name was more likely the result of an amal-
gamation of two inns. Moreover the most attractive sign,
a portrait surrounded by eight handbells, shows a greater
likeness to Charles I than to Charles II.

All England's rivers have their inns. Their heyday has

passed but they still serve refreshment, though less now to the watermen than to the general public who watch the bustle of the river while enjoying their drink.

When the canal era set in, dating mainly from the industrial revolution, inns very soon sprang up beside them, particularly at locks and convenient stopping places, and enjoyed an all too brief prosperity. Unfortunately, history repeated itself and with the decline of traffic on the inland waterways many faded away, but there are still quite a number left close to the tow paths of the canals still in use.

On the Grand Union Canal is the *Black Horse*, which adjoins the famous staircase of ten locks at Foxton, Market Harborough. This was designed to lift canal traffic some 83 ft within a distance of half-a-mile, and the remains of the old steam lift can still be seen. Also on the Grand Union are the *North Bridge*, within a stone's throw of the shops in Leicester; the *Plough*, with its canal-side gardens; the *Fishery*, Foxton, Market Harborough, and many others which have been able to adapt to the new-style traffic.

Other attractive canal inns include: *Three Horseshoes, Cowroast*, nr Tring (Herts); *Paddington Packet*, between Paddington and Uxbridge; *Row Barge*; *Grand Junction*; and *Boat & Horses*. Most numerous of all are the *Navigations*, which are to be found on most of the waterways. The Trent and Mersey canal has a *Romping Donkey* and a *Plum Pudding* and on the straight mile of the same canal there is the *Potter's Arms*, in the very centre of an area closely associated with the early days of the potteries. The *Big Lock*, Middlewich (Cheshire), stands by the lock of that name, and in days gone by its stables were much in demand to house the bargees' horses. Near Garston (Yorks) the *Anchor* is still in business close by one of the canal locks and at Acaster Malbis, nr York, where the *Ship* stands on the river bank, one can still see the hole where beer was passed through to the bargees who took a quick drink without stopping their horses.

Some inns have tenaciously held on to life, even though the canal by which they stood has become disused or derelict. An instance is *Tunnel House*, nr Coates (Glos), which was built to house the men building this section of the Thames/Severn canal in 1783. The canal here passes through a legging tunnel—traversed by barges propelled by men's feet on the tunnel roof—and the inn later became a rendezvous for the men in charge of the barge horses, who led them over the hill to await the arrival of the barges at the far end of the tunnel. As with the roadside inns which managed to hold on between the end of the coaching era and the coming of the motor-car, so *Tunnel House* survived and is now a popular port of call for summer visitors. Other such inns, it is to be hoped, will also take on a new lease of life now that many of our canals are being re-opened for pleasure boating.

The signs used to denote inns and other kinds of businesses could well have received their death knell when the naming of streets and numbering of houses became general early in the nineteenth century. Fortunately, the very opposite happened, and many streets were named after the inn which had been there even before the street. Examples of this abound in most of the older towns and cities. Well known is Half Moon Street, Piccadilly, London, which took the name of the 'local'. When the Croydon Railway was opened in 1839, many of the stations were named after inns that had long been popular on the route the line followed. *New Cross*, *Dartmouth Arms*, *Anerley Arms* and *Jolly Sailor* were some of them. The last unlikely name for a station was changed to 'Norwood Junction' in 1846. Yet another station example is the 'Elephant & Castle,' London, which obviously derived its name from the famous tavern which stood there until a few years ago.

The Railways

WHEN the railways superseded the coaches and the canals, many inn signs were changed to be 'in tune' with the new method of travelling. Quite numerous, though not very original, were the *Railway* hotels, inns or taverns. Later, some of the early steam engines were depicted on signs as, for instance, a 'Puffing Billy' at *The Railway*, Ross-on-Wye, (Herefs), and the 'North Star of 1837', which features on the sign of the *Great Western Arms*, Warwick. Many of the really great engines have achieved lasting fame on signs, including the *Royal Scot*, Carlisle (Cumb), and *Silver Bullet*, Finsbury Park, London. Commemorated, too, are 'crack' trains such as the 'Golden Arrow', with its fine two-sided sign on the Golden Valley Estate, Folkestone (Kent), and 'The Torbay Express', which is pictured on the sign of the *Railway*, Newton Abbot (Devon).

Justice is more than done outside Spennymoor Station (Co Durham) for there are three inns—the *Station*, the *North-Eastern* and the *Railway*—the latter having a reproduction of the 'Comet' on its board.

Other examples of railway nostalgia include such names as *Light Railway*, Hulme End (Staffs), which commemorates the line which ran from Leek through the Manifold Valley to Hulme End from 1904-34. Similarly, the *Cheshire Lines*, Southport (Lancs), recalls the branch line which once ran from Cheshire to Southport.

There is an *Engine & Tender*, at St Neots (Hunts), and a milestone in railway history is commemorated at the *George & Dragon*, Yarm (Yorks) where a plaque informs:

'In the Commercial Rooms of this Hotel on the 12th day of February, 1820, was held the Promoters Meeting of the Stockton and Darlington Railway, the First Public Railway in the World. Thomas Meynell, Esq., of Yarm presided'

The table and chairs used on that occasion are still retained in a room of the inn.

In the same way that coach services and railways have left their mark on inn signs, so has that twentieth-century invention, the aeroplane. Among the many signs of aero-nautical interest are : the *Propeller,* near London Airport and the *Flying Lancaster,* renamed from the *Lancaster,* Desford (Leics). *Canopus,* Rochester (Kent) takes its name from the first of the 'Empire' class flying-boats built and launched by Short Bros at Rochester in 1936 and *Comet,* at Hatfield (Herts), similarly commemorates a famous product of the nearby De Havilland company.

At Brough, on the Humber estuary, there is a *Buccaneer,* named after the Fleet Air Arm's fighter-bomber, and at Bristol the *Wayfarer* reminds us of another locally-built aircraft. There is also a *Wellington* at Hastings, a *Walrus* at Plymouth, and a very attractive *Jet & Whittle* sign at Gloucester, where the famous Whittle-engined aircraft were built.

Heraldic Signs

A GREAT number of present-day signs have sprung from some form of heraldry, although very often we could be forgiven for not immediately recognising the association. Royal arms or badges of nobility had a particular attraction to loyal and patriotic Englishmen, with the result that all kinds of heraldic animals appear today on our signboards. The lion first made its appearance in the badges of William I and William II, and the following is a rough guide to some of the others:

Blue Boar and *White Boar* were both badges of the House of York but after the defeat of Richard at the battle of Bosworth, the blue boars on inn signs were hastily coloured white by innkeepers anxious to be on the winning side. The blue boars appear to have been particularly fierce animals, judging by the many signs of the name in Warwickshire and Oxfordshire. The *Blue Boar*, Chipping Norton (Oxon), is fiercer than most.

Red Rose, emblem of the Lancastrians, was always popular and the *White Rose* represented the Yorkists.

Rose & Crown also came from the Wars of the Roses, and symbolised the marriage of Henry VII to Elizabeth, daughter of Edward IV—a marriage which brought to a close the wars that had been raging up and down the country for thirty years.

White Lion appeared in the badge of Edward IV.

Blue Lion. Signs with the lion are legion, for they have appeared in the arms of monarchs of England since Henry I in the twelfth century. The blue lion was also associated with the Prince of Denmark who was the

Consort of Queen Anne. The black variety was associated with Queen Philippa, Consort of Edward III.

Golden Lion represented the Lion of Flanders.

Falcon was another Yorkist sign. It also appeared in the crest of Queen Elizabeth I.

Greyhound. Still a very popular sign, of which a small number only can be attributed to the sport of greyhound racing. The earliest historical greyhound signs obviously came from the badge of the Tudors.

Dragon. Another sign which came largely from heraldry. It appears on the eleventh-century Bayeaux tapestry and was later included in the arms of the Tudors. The *Red Dragon* usually refers to Wales.

Tabard. Quite a popular sign, deriving from the sleeveless tunic worn by heralds.

White Hart was a much favoured sign in earlier centuries. It was the badge of Richard II and his popularity undoubtedly led to its frequent adoption. There is a *White Hart* to be found in most market towns.

Unicorn was brought into the royal arms by James I, and was the Scottish unicorn.

White Horse. Far more popular than the monarchs who were responsible for it being used as an inn sign, the white horse was brought to this country as a badge by the Hanoverian kings.

Swan was in the arms of Henry V.

Raven featured in the arms of Mary I.

Red Lion, of which there are several hundred in the country, undoubtedly came mainly from John of Gaunt's badge. The son of Edward III and father of Henry IV, he was the most powerful figure in the realm for some thirty years. At least two inns are named after him, *John of Gaunt*, Lancaster, and *John of Gaunt*, Rothwell (W.R. Yorks).

Whilst it would be wrong to assume that all inn signs bearing these animals derived from the royal arms, they no doubt owed their inception to them, although in later years there may have been other reasons for adopting an animal sign.

Royal Signs

THE Englishman's traditional affection for his monarch is reflected in such signs as the *Crown*, of which there are well over 1,000 in all parts of the country.

Many early kings are also represented on signs. The Saxon king, Ethelbert, who ascended the throne in 860, is remembered by *King Ethelbert*, Herne Bay (Kent). There are several of *King Alfred*, and others include *Canute* and *Harold*. William the Conqueror is represented, as is his brother Robert de Mortain, on signs appropriately in Sussex, and there is a *Norman King* at Dunstable (Beds). Such signs are usually isolated instances relating to a particular monarch, and the inn so-named is likely to be in the vicinity of some place associated with him. The *Rufus* in the New Forest—close to where the king was killed by an arrow—is a case in point. There is also a *King John*, Tollard Royal (Wilts) and an *Old King John*, Hastings (Sussex). There is an *Edward II* at Merriott (Som) and *Richard III* is proclaimed by signs at Greenwich and Leicester. Elizabeth I, Mary I, and Mary Queen of Scots, James I (James II appears nowhere), Charles I, William and Mary, Anne, William IV, Victoria, Edward VII, George V and our present Queen Elizabeth II are all represented by inn signs. In fact, most kings and queens of England since the fifteenth century appear on signs, with Henry VIII by far the most common of the earlier ones. Whether this was due to his popularity or because there were many famous portraits of him which could easily be copied, is open to conjecture.

Charles II also has a very good showing, usually represented in hiding in hundreds of *Royal Oaks*, in the course of his escape from the battle of Worcester. *Rose Revived* is sometimes an allusion to the Restoration, and at the *King's Arms*, Ockley (Surrey), the gay monarch is depicted on the sign with his arm round Nell Gwyn, perhaps the most endearing of his numerous mistresses.

Frequently a monarch's portrait appears on the sign but the name of the inn is either the *King's* or *Queen's Head* or *Arms*. These are common all over the country.

Inns named after a particular monarch whose likeness is displayed on the sign, include:

HENRY VI, at Islington, London and believed to be the only one.

HENRY VIII, generally after the Holbein portrait, as at the *King's Head*, nr Gloucester, and at Chepstow (Mon).

CHARLES I, whose execution aroused a wide measure of public sympathy. There are not so many now as in earlier years. A good likeness is at Kettlewell (Yorks).

ELIZABETH I. The *Queen Elizabeth*, Chingford (Essex) has her likeness as on a coin.

JAMES I. Several inns show the monarch with the title of *King's Head* but another ascribed to him is *Three Crowns*, Tysoe Street, London, W.1, as he was the first to rule over the three kingdoms.

QUEEN ANNE is not so popular as one would have imagined. She is represented on the sign of the *Queen*, London, S.W.8.

EDWARD VII, a rare one. At Littleton (Worcs) he is shown on the sign in his coronation robes. The likeness could easily be taken for George V.

GEORGE. This is a very popular sign but rarely does it depict any particular Hanoverian king. As they all looked alike, to most people, this does not really matter. There are, however, some exceptions. A particularly good sign at Chideock (Dorset) shows George II on the battlefield at Dettingen, when the French were defeated in 1743. George II had the distinction of being the last of our kings to take an active part in battle. At Birdlip (Glos) is a *Royal George*, the sign depicting George III as he was late in life; and in Portugal Street, London, there is *George IV*, with a facsimile of a coin bearing his likeness.

WILLIAM IV was admired by his subjects, so that there are many reminders of him. *Royal William*, Cranham (Glos), and *Royal Sailor* also refer to him.

WILLIAM AND MARY is usually found under the sign or name of *King & Queen*. As the only royal couple to jointly hold the Crown, it is strange they are not more numerous. A Whitbread sign at Mottingham, London, carries a portrait of Mary only.

VICTORIA appears in various phases of her life. Sometimes as the very young queen at the commencement of her reign, as on the large and handsomely coloured sign at Windermere (Westm). Also in the Lake District she is depicted on a sign as on a 'penny black' stamp. At Gloucester are portraits of both the coronation period and the jubilee period. A similar sign adorns the *Jubilee*, Folkestone (Kent). A few signs show her as a grim-faced widow and a number of others, depicting the queen with her consort, are usually found at inns bearing the name of *Victoria & Albert*.

GEORGE V has his likeness on the sign of the *Ordinary Fellow*, Chatham (Kent). This is a quotation of the king's words when he was overcome by the acclamation of the crowds at his jubilee.

GEORGE VI appears on the *Five Alls* sign, Cheltenham (Glos), as does our present queen on a similar sign of the *Four Alls*, Ovington (Yorks).

ELIZABETH II's portrait is the sign of the *Queen's Head*, Workington (Cumb).

Of the many signs commemorating Princes of the Blood, the *Prince of Wales* is easily the most numerous and there are also many *Feathers* which refer to his crest. A large number of inns are named after the sons of the Georges, including: *Duke of York*, *Prince Regent*, *Duke of Cambridge*, *Duke of Kent*, and *Prince George*. Queen Victoria's numerous family are also well represented with *Duke of Clarence*, *Duke of Edinburgh*, *Prince Leopold*, *Prince Arthur*, *Princess Royal* and *Princess Alice*. There is a rare sign of the latter, bearing the likeness of the Princess, at Forest Gate, London. *Prince Albert* and *Prince Consort* are frequently-met reminders of Queen Victoria's husband and there is a particularly good portrait sign of him at Rodborough (Glos).

There are a variety of other patriotic signs, including *Royal Standard*, *King's Arms*, *Crown & Sceptre*, and, not least those which show the patron saint of England fighting the dragon. Sometimes the sign pictures the full tableau though the inn is just the *George*, as at Guildford (Surrey). At other places, such as Uldale (Cumb), it is the *George & Dragon* and a very fine sign this small inn exhibits.

Page 35 : An excellent, and now historical sign at Wellington (Herefordshire)

Page 36 : One of many signs commemorating Sir Winston Churchill.
This, appropriately, is at Churchill (Somerset)

Royal houses other than the English get a fair showing in names of inns. Mary Queen of Scots is sometimes identified as *Scottish Queen*, and also figures on the *Queen's Head* at Stratford-upon-Avon (Warws). At Finsbury, London, the *Empress of Russia* refers to Catherine the Great who, born the daughter of a Lithuanian peasant, reigned from 1684 to 1727. *Queen Catherine*, Osmotherley (Yorks) serves as a memorial to Catherine Parr, sixth and last wife of Henry VIII, who is reputed to have had some association with Osmotherley.

Prominent familes also have their coats of arms on signs in many parts of the country, particularly in areas where in days gone by they had estates. The arms of the Duke of Devonshire are to be found in Yorkshire, Derbyshire and elsewhere, the *Marlborough Arms* in many areas and the *Beaufort Arms* in Cheltenham (Glos). The splendid colouring of many of these family coats of arms makes them very attractive signs and two particularly good examples are to be seen at the *Redesdale Arms*, Moreton-in-Marsh (Glos) and the *Stansfield Arms*, Burley (Yorks). The lineage of the Stansfield family dates back to the Conquest and the sign, the work of Ronald Kitchen, is a glorious piece of English pageantry set against a background of castle and moorland.

These family coats of arms are apt to appear in the most unexpected places without any obvious connection with the family concerned. In Cornwall, near Hayle, for example, there is a small village called Leeds Town whose inn, *Duke of Leeds*, has as its sign the arms of the family which inherited, through marriage, the nearby Godolphin estates.

Often sections or even symbols from a family coat of arms are used as inn signs. Thus the eagle often represents the Earls of Derby, and the talbot (a dog) the Earls of Shrewsbury. Another popular sign was the *Blue Boar* as the badge of

c

the de Vere family, while the *Bear & Ragged Staff* was taken from that of the Earls of Warwick.

Less aristocratic families also have their arms and names represented on inn signs, again generally at inns within the area of their once large estates.

The Illustrious and Famous

BY far the greatest number of signs named after people commemorate illustrious or famous characters who, for some reason or another, endeared themselves to the British public. By their numbers we can today gain some idea of the affection in which they were held at the time of their achievements. Lord Nelson easily leads the field in this category, followed closely by Wellington. The following list is no more than representative and embraces only a small fraction of the many such names which are to be found.

The list is arranged alphabetically for convenience but the names of the inns often take the form of the title as well as the name of the personality, i.e. *General Allenby*. Where specific signs and their location are mentioned it does not necessarily follow that they are unique.

ALLENBY, General (1861-1936). Nr Wimborne (Dorset). Captured Jerusalem in the 1914-18 war.

ALTEN, General Von (1764-1840). Chatham. Remembers a German general who was an ally of Britain, for Karl von Alten commanded a German legion in British service during the Napoleonic war.

AMHURST, Sir Geoffrey (1717-97). A soldier, who from a

pageboy to the Duke of Dorset rose to be Field Marshal. Born at Riverhead (Kent), a fact which is remembered at Higtham nearby, where the *Sir Geoffrey Amhurst* commemorates him.

BEATTY, Earl (1871-1936). Admiral 1914-18 war, Motspur Park, London, and *Admiral Beatty*, Leicester.

BRIDGEWATER, Duke of (1763-1803). *Bridgewater Arms*, Stockport (Cheshire). He constructed the first major canal in Britain.

BRUNSWICK, Duke of (1771-1815). Entered the British Service and fought in the Peninsular war. Killed at Waterloo.

BULLER, Sir Redvers (1839-1908). *Bullers Arms*. Several named after him in Devon and Cornwall. He raised the siege of Ladysmith in the South African war, 1900. He lived near Exeter.

CAMDEN, William (1551-1623). Bexley Heath (Kent). Born in London, became a great scholar, antiquary and historian. He wrote the great survey of the British Isles, 'Britannia', in 1586.

CANNING, Earl (1812-62). Hartpury (Glos) and elsewhere. Was Governor-General of India and played an important part in quelling the Indian Mutiny.

CLYDE, Lord—Sir Colin Campbell (1792-1863). Created a baron after suppression of the Indian Mutiny. Inn sign popular in the North of England.

CODRINGTON, Admiral (1770-1855) London, S.W.3. Joined the Navy at the age of thirteen. Led a squadron at Trafalgar in 1805. Took a leading part in the Battle of Navarino, which destroyed the Turkish Navy in 1827.

COTTON, Charles (1630-87) (Derbys). Poet and friend of Izaac Walton. Born in Beresford (Staffs). A brilliant and versatile genius.

CROMWELL, Oliver, Lord Protector from 1653-58. *Oliver Cromwell*, and *Cromwell's Head*, Cheltenham (Glos). The first named would seem a tribute, the second jubilation.

CROMWELL, Richard (1626-1712). He was the son of the great Protector, but was not taken seriously by the British public. However, there are one or two signs which identify him under the name of *Happy Dick*; 'Happy' presumably, because he avoided the cares of state. The inn of this name at Abingdon (Berks) is now closed but there are others about the country. Another reference to him is the sign *Tumbledown Dick*, but as there was a popular old English dance of this name, there is no certainty that it perpetuates the memory of this unfortunate young man.

CUMBERLAND, William, Duke of (1721-65). *Duke William* and *Duke of Cumberland*. Second son of George II. He had a distinguished military career. Crushed the rebellion of the Young Pretender at Culloden. For his cruelty, he was known north of the border as the 'barbarous butcher'.

CUNNINGHAM, General Sir Alan (b. 1887). Bracknell (Berks). A great military leader and one of the first of the generals of World War II to appear on a sign.

DARNLEY, Lord (1545-67). Near Holyrood Palace, Edinburgh. Husband of Mary Queen of Scots.

ELLIOTT, General (1717-90). Leeds and Uxbridge (Middx). He was a distinguished soldier and hero of Gibraltar, which he defended against the Spaniards in 1779-83. He was created 1st Baron Heathfield.

EXMOUTH, Lord (1757-1833). Had a distinguished naval career and destroyed the pirates' stronghold at Algiers. Numerous signs, mostly displaying his arms, as at Cheltenham (Glos) and Exmouth (Devon).

FAZAKERLEY, Nicholas (d. 1767). Chorley (Lancs). Lawyer and politician. He was Member of Parliament for Preston and a Jacobite.

FITZWILLIAM, Earl (1786-1857). Near Rotherham (Yorks). He was one of the earliest advocates of Free Trade.

FREDERICK the Great (1712-86). *King of Prussia*, a popular sign but in many cases from 1914 onwards for patriotic reasons, 'Prussia' became 'Russia'. He was the son of a daughter of George I.

GARRICK, David (1717-79). *Garrick's Head* or *Garrick*, are two versions of the signs to this famous eighteenth-century actor who is buried in Westminster Abbey.

GORDON, General Charles (1833-85). Gordon of Khartoum.

GORDON, George. One of the earlier chiefs of the Gordon clan. A variety of signs in Scotland to his memory include: *Heiland Laddie, Cock o' the North, Gay Gordon* and *Huntly Arms*.

GRANBY, Marquis of (1721-70). Distinguished soldier who was very popular with the troops. Fought at Minden (1759) and Warburg (1760). Signs all over the country from Surrey to Derbyshire are due to his having set up many of his wounded senior non-commissioned officers in their own inns, a contributary cause of the £37,000 of debts he left at his death.

HAIG, Earl (1861-1928). Field Marshal 1914-18 war. Hertford (Herts) and Hounslow (Middx).

HARDY, Admiral, Thomas Masterman (1769-1839). London S.E.10. Nelson's Hardy. Governor of Greenwich Hospital.

HARVEY, Admiral Sir Eliab (1758-1830). Dover (Kent). Commanded the *Temeraire* at Trafalgar.

HAVELOCK, General Sir Henry (1795-1857). Served in Afghanistan campaign and Indian Mutiny. Died of dysentry. Good signs at Hastings (Sussex), Burnley (Lancs) and elsewhere.

HAWKINS, Sir John (1532-95). *Hawkins Arms* (Cornwall) Honours the sea-dog who helped to beat the Armada.

HOLLAND, Henry (1746-1806). London, W.1. Architect who designed Battersea Bridge, Brooks Club, Brighton Pavilion, Drury Lane Theatre, etc.

HOOD, Lord (1724-1816). London, E.1. Admiral and a contemporary of Rodney.

JACKSON, Ward (1806-80). West Hartlepool (Co. Durham). This is a good example of a local philanthropist being honoured by an inn sign. He was chairman of the Hartlepool & Stockton Railway and responsible for building the harbour and dock, which marked the beginning of West Hartlepool in 1847. He was Member of Parliament for Hartlepool, 1868-74.

JOHNSON, Doctor Samuel (1709-84). Barkingside (Essex). He was the famous lexicographer.

JONSON, Ben (1572-1637). Wigan (Lancs). Dramatist and poet. Friend of Shakespeare and Bacon.

KEPPEL, Admiral (1725-86). There are several prominent soldiers and sailors with this name. The admiral accompanied Anson in a voyage round the world in 1740 and, after a distinguished career, was created Viscount.

KYRLE, John (1637-1724). *Man of Ross*, Ross-on-Wye (Herefs). He was a great local benefactor.

LANGTON, Stephen (1150-1228). Friday Street (Surrey). Archbishop of Canterbury. Famous theologian and historian.

LAWRENCE, Sir John (1811-79). New Southgate, London. A great administrator in India and Viceroy from 1864 until 1868.

LIND, Jenny (1820-87). Sutton (Surrey). Real name Madam Goldschmidt, the great soprano singer, who was known in Britain as the 'Swedish Nightingale'. Very religious, much loved and admired by the public, she died at Malvern (Worcs).

LIVINGSTONE, Dr David (1813-73). Great missionary, traveller and explorer. Discovered the Victoria Falls, Zambezi and Lake Nyasa. The *Livingstone*, Birkenhead, follows the name of the street named after him. The decor of the house follows an African theme.

LONDONDERRY, 3rd Marquis of (1778-1854). Brilliant soldier but the *Lord Seaham* (his name before becoming Marquis) remembers him at Hetton-le-Hole (Co. Durham) for the great improvements he carried out to the area around his estates, including the opening of collieries, building of the harbour, docks and railway.

LORD, Thomas. West Meon (Hants). Famous eighteenth-century ornithologist.

LORNE, Marquis of (1678-1743). Wallsend (Northumb) and elsewhere in the North. He distinguished himself under Marlborough.

MACBRIDE, Admiral. Plymouth (Devon). A famous admiral who served under Rodney and was also Member of Parliament for Plymouth from 1784 to 1790.

MARLBOROUGH, Duke of (1650-1722). Hero of Blenheim. Numerous signs. There are also many of the family name generally.

MONMOUTH, James Duke of (1649-85). Illegitimate son of Charles I and Lucy Walters. Led rebellion against James II, landing at Lyme Regis (Dorset) where *Ye Olde Monmouth* perpetuates his name.

MONTFORT, Simon de (1208-65). Leicester. Leader of the Barons' Revolt.

MOUNTBATTEN, Lord Louis. The sign at Poole (Dorset) refers to the present Lord Mountbatten, who officially opened the house in 1960. It depicts the family coat of arms. The *Milford Haven* (Pembs) is in memory of Prince Louis Mountbatten (1854-1921), who was also an Admiral of the Fleet.

NAPIER, Lord (1810-90). Blackburn (Lancs). Great soldier of the Indian Mutiny and the Chinese War.

NEWTON, Sir Isaac (1642-1727). Grantham (Lincs). He attended Grantham Grammar School and in 1686 discovered the law of gravity.

ORANGE, William of. *Prince of Orange* refers to William II, father of William III of England.

OWEN, Admiral Sir Edward (1771-1849). Sandwich (Kent).

PAXTON, Sir Joseph (1801-65). Tichfield (Hants). He was an architect and gardener who started life as a lad on the Duke of Devonshire's Chatsworth estate, where he re-modelled the gardens. Later designed the Crystal Palace.

PEEL, John (1776-1854). A Cumberland huntsman for fifty years and renowned through the song, 'D'ye ken John Peel?' Quite a popular sign, especially in the Lake District.

PEEL, Sir Robert (1788-1850). London, E.C.2 and Leicester. Eminent nineteenth-century politician. Founder of the modern police force.

PEPYS, Samuel (1633-1703). Gillingham (Kent). He was the famous diarist, and Secretary of the Navy.

RAGLAN, Lord (1788-1855). Great soldier who lost an arm at Waterloo, and commanded troops at the Crimea.

RALEIGH, Sir Walter (1552-1618). Dartmouth and East Budleigh (Devon). Strange that this great Elizabethan is not featured more often.

RAWDON, General Sir George (1604-84). Fought under Monck in the Irish Rebellion. Supported the Restoration. He was born at Leeds (Yorks) and a sign, probably the only one, is at Luddenden Foot (W.R. Yorks).

REMBRANDT, (1606-69). Manchester. The great Dutch artist.

REYNOLDS, Sir Joshua (1732-92). The greatest of all English portrait painters. Born at Plympton (Devon) where the inn named after him is situated. He was at the height of his fame at the early age of thirty-seven.

RODNEY, Lord (1719-92). *Bold Rodney, Lord Rodney, Rodney's Head*. Admiral. A very popular figure, judging by the number of signs in his honour.

ROSCO, Sir Henry (1833-1915). Liverpool. He was educated at Liverpool and was Professor of Chemistry at Manchester and Liberal Member of Parliament for South Manchester.

ROY, Rob (Gaelic: Red Robert) (1671-1734). Scottish 'Robin Hood'. Many signs of him in the Trossachs and Loch Lomond areas of Scotland.

RUSSELL, Earl (1792-1878). Bristol. He was a nineteenth-century politician and became Prime Minister in 1865.

RUSSELL, Jack (1795-1883). Swimbridge (Devon). The clergyman who was vicar of a remote North Devon village and became famous as a foxhunting squire. He bred the original Jack Russell terrier. A great huntsman, he was in the field up to the end of his life. A thousand people from all walks of life attended his funeral. The inn has recently been renamed from 'New Inn' in his honour.

SIDDONS, Sarah (1755-1831). Cheltenham (Glos). The sign on a modern house, built on the site of a former theatre where this great actress was said to have performed.

SNOW, John (1813-58). London, W.1. The doctor who discovered in 1844 that cholera was spread by contaminated water. He also introduced scientific use of ether into English surgical practice.

SUTHERLAND, Duchess of (1806-68). Holloway, London. She was Mistress of the Robes and a great friend of Queen Victoria.

TALMA (1763-1826). London. Famous French actor who enjoyed considerable success in London.

TARLETON, General (1754-1833). Fought in the American War of Independence. Was also Member of Parliament for Liverpool (1790-1806). Signs at Newcastle and Ferrensby (W.R. Yorks).

TRURO, Lord (1782-1855). Dalston, London. Lord Chancellor. Defended Queen Caroline at the celebrated trial. One of the earliest supporters of Rowland Hill's postal reforms.

TYRRELL, Sir Walter. New Forest (Hants). The man who is alleged to have killed William II (Rufus) in the New Forest in 1100.

VERMUYDEN, Sir Cornelius (1595-1683). Dutch engineer, who was given a grant by Charles I to drain Lincolnshire and Yorkshire marshes. The Dutch river, an artificial mouth of the river Don, was so-named as a tribute to his skill. The inn bearing his name is by the Dutch river in Yorkshire.

VERNON, Admiral (1684-1757). The popularity of the sign is probably because he was the first to issue 'grog'—rum diluted with water—to the Navy. He was cashiered from the Service in 1746.

WADE, General (1673-1748). (Leeds). Sent to Scotland in 1724 as Commander-in-Chief and was responsible for the construction of important military roads and forty stone bridges, which brought the north and west of Scotland into touch with the rest of the British Isles. Started the work in 1726, using 500 soldiers who received 6d per day extra. Wade retired to Leeds and nearby the inn is Wade Lane. The inn, a new one and octagonal in shape, is situated in Wade Lane.

WALMESLEY, Sir Thomas (1537-1612). Billington (Lancs). Born at nearby Rishton. A prominent judge and a man of great learning.

WEBB, Matthew (1849-83). Known as Captain Webb, he swam the Channel in 1875, when he was in the water twenty-two hours and swam forty miles. Using the breast stroke all the time, he did not touch a boat for the whole period. He died trying to swim through the rapids of Niagara Falls. The *Captain Webb*, Wellington (Salop) near his birthplace, contains photographs and mementos of his Channel swim.

WHITTINGTON, Richard (d. 1423). *Whittington Stone*, Highgate (London), *Whittington Cat*, Whitehaven, (Cumb). Several inns bear the name honouring the Gloucestershire boy who became Lord Mayor of London in the fifteenth century, and was reputed to have had a famous cat.

WOLFE, General (1727-59). Ramsgate (Kent) and Penrith (Cumb). He had a distinguished military career. Commanded the British force which scaled the heights of Abraham, Quebec, but was killed at the moment of victory over the French.

By the nineteenth century the field of interest had widened considerably—historical events, kings and queens, great soldiers, sailors, statesmen and especially sporting events, all had their share of the ever-growing number of lively and attractive signs.

The names of politicians, too, began to appear on inn signs as, for instance, *Earl Grey*, *Lord Morpeth*, Disraeli *(Beaconsfield Arms)*, *Sir Robert Peel*, *Sir Francis Burdett*, *Cobden*, *John Burns*, *Earl Fitzwilliam*, *Gladstone* (one doubts if he would have approved); *Lambton*, John George; *William Pitt*, Lloyd George *(Pride of the Valley)* Churt (Surrey); *Earl Russell* and scores more.

Then came scientists and inventors, led by *William Caxton*, the father of English printing, and followed by *Sir Isaac Newton*, *John Baird* and *Sir David Brewster*. William Willet, the originator of daylight saving, is remembered by the *Daylight* inn, Petts Wood (Kent) his home, and also in Essex.

Great liberators featured include *William Tell*, Louis Kossuth (*The Independent*, London, N.1) and *Garibaldi*, while *Captain Cook* is among the explorers. *Tom Cribb* heads the prizefighters and W. G. Grace (*The Yorker*, London, W.1) leads the field in cricket.

Some of the most unlikely people still appear on inn signs. Among prelates there is *Thomas á Becket*, *Cardinal Wolsey* and, at Chudleigh (Devon), *Bishop Lacy*. *Saint Alban* is at Cheltenham (Glos), *Saint Wilfred* at Ripon (Yorks), and *Bishop Blaise*, the patron saint of woolcombers, is understandably popular in the North Country. Innerleithen (Peebles) has its *St Ronan* and near Thirlemere (Cumb) there is *St John's in the Vale*.

From saints to sinners, and what more glamorous example than 'pretty witty' *Nell Gwyn*, whose memory is perpetuated at Southsea (Hants) and Chelsea, London. Twice remembered, too, is a man who was more feared in the nineteenth century than was Hitler in the twentieth, Napoleon Bonaparte, with one *Napoleon* at Guildford (Surrey) and another at Boscastle (Cornwall).

PART TWO

The Origin of some Unusual and Popular Signs

Axe & Compass represents the arms of the Company of Carpenters and is typical of the once numerous signs of trade.

Baccanals was the name given to many inns and derives from Bacchanalia, the feasts and orgies of Bacchus, god of wine. Centuries of mispronunciation resulted in the present rendering 'Bag o' Nails'.

Bell: more than 500 inns bear this name. The early ones were usually near the cathedral or parish church.

Bible & Crown comes from the Civil War when the words were the favourite toast of the Cavaliers. During the Parliament, discretion was the better part of valour and nearly all of them disappeared.

Bull & Mouth: believed originally to have been 'Boulogne Mouth', which commemorated the capture of Boulogne by Henry VIII in 1544.

Swan with Two Necks is believed to have arisen from a misconception, the word 'nicks' being understood as 'necks'. The Vintner's Company marked their swans with two nicks on the bill as a sign of ownership.

Case is Altered: several theories are advanced for this name. One is that it referred to an inn formerly on the site of a nunnery at Woodbridge (Suffolk), which a

Father Casey used to visit for confessions. A garbled version became 'Casey's Altar' and then the 'Case is Altered'. Another more probable story is that when the 57th Regiment of Foot returned from the Peninsular War with smatterings of Spanish, the term 'Casar de Salta', meaning perhaps a type of dance, was freely used. Again, pronunciation over the years became 'Case is Altered'. The last version is the story attached to the house of that name at Harrow (Middx).

St Peter's Finger is a famous sign at Lychett Minster (Dorset). It was believed to be the nearest the country-man could get to St Peter ad Vincula, whose feast was celebrated close by. The sign could also be interpreted as the Pope's finger raised in blessing.

Leg & Star: derived from the insignia of the Garter.

Blue Ball, in days gone by, was the sign of a fortune-teller. Blue is a favourite colour for inn signs and there are two score or more of blue subjects, ranging from Gainsborough's 'Blue Boy' to Blue Dogs.

Bull is a sign almost certain to be found in every market town and certainly every city. Whilst some stemmed from family crests, the vast majority came from the Englishman's once favourite sport of bull-baiting. Usually the bull was tethered to an iron ring in the market place and dogs were set on the unfortunate animal. The stone to which the bull was tethered is still to be seen on the roadway outside the former *Bay Horse*, Skipton (Yorks).

Many inns also had a bear pit and agitation against the great cruelty involved in both pursuits went on for half a century before Parliament passed a law forbidding bull-baiting in 1836. The bull is often found in strange company for there is a *Bull & Swan* and even a *Bull in the Oak*.

Cross Keys, prior to the Reformation, was a very common sign and represented the emblem of St Peter. When Henry VIII broke with Rome, a number of the signs changed to the *King's Head*.

Green Man: a common sign in some counties, it represented the forester, and was sometimes meant to portray Robin Hood. Often too, it sprang from folk lore. Another form of the sign is *Jack-in-the-Green*, a prominent figure in pagan revels.

Greyhound: this sign is still frequently seen and dates from the time of the Tudors, who used it as a badge and on their coat of arms. Until late in the eighteenth century a silver greyhound was worn on the sleeve of the King's messengers. Sometimes it has a sporting association.

Leather Bottle: a container made of leather was the earliest type of receptacle for ale or wine, hence the popularity of the sign. One of the original containers is in the Guildhall Museum.

Black Jack: another sign named after a drinking vessel of former days.

Pack Horse is a reminder of the days when pack animals were the only form of transport and merchants and travellers represented a large proportion of the innkeepers' trade.

Pig & Whistle: a very old sign of which there are still a number. It is thought to have been adapted from the Saxon *piggen* (milking pail) and *wassail* (be in health). In early days beer was served in pails and customers dipped their mugs, called 'pigs' and served themselves. Another suggested origin is that it was originally 'Pige-Washail', the first two words in Anglo-Saxon of the Angel's Salutation to the Virgin Mary.

Punch Bowl was a political sign introduced at the end of the seventeenth century, when punch became the fashionable drink. Punch was a Whig drink, whilst the Tories adhered to sack, claret and canary. Hence it followed that 'The Punch Bowl' became the sign of taverns patronised by Whigs.

Ram is a fairly common sign in clothmaking districts, for it is the crest of the Worshipful Company of Cloth Workers. It is not exclusive to the North Country but can also be seen in other areas of England. There is one such sign in the city of Gloucester, close to which the Huguenots settled in the sixteenth century. A similar sign is the *Ram & Teazle*, the teazle having been used in the processing of cloth. The *Ram's Head* is also fairly common.

Bird in Hand: most of these signs stem from the medieval sport of hawking, when the bird is held on the hand.

Bush, from earliest times, indicated a drinking house. The vine has the same significance.

Catherine Wheel is believed to have been adapted from the badge of the Knights of St Catherine of Mount Sinai, an order founded in the eleventh century to protect pilgrims on their journey to the Holy Sepulchre.

Gate is still quite a common sign, and most are on or near the former site of a toll gate. One of the best known is *The Gate Hangs Well*, Syston (Leics). The sign is a five-bar gate carrying the legend :

> This Gate Hangs Well
> and Hinders none
> Refresh and pay
> and Travel on.

Halfway House: these are also numerous though, with changes in road systems, many are today only halfway

Page 53 : Playing cards make attractive signs; (*top*) Highworth (Wilts);
(*bottom left*) Bradford; (*bottom right*) Newcastle (Staffs)

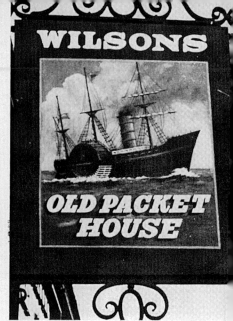

Page 54: Four forms of transport; (*top left*) Huddersfield; (*top right*) Altrincham (Cheshire); (*centre*) Stratford - on - Avon; (*bottom*) *Travellers Rest*, Grasmere (Westmorland)

between two insignificant points, instead of, as formerly, between two important towns.

Hop Pole: when a hop pole was displayed with a wreath of hops on the end, it indicated that a new brew was ready for tasting by the official ale taster.

Hole in the Wall: all sorts of theories are advanced as to the origin of this name and the most reasonable explanation is that the inn was situated off the pathway in a snug corner, approached perhaps by an alley.

New Inn: when a new building was erected on the site of an old one, it naturally became the 'New' inn. Today 'New' inns are often among the most ancient, at any rate so far as the site of an inn is concerned.

Ring o' Bells, deriving from the Englishman's love of handbell ringing, was a very popular sign, particularly in country districts where the sign is generally to be found. At *Eight Bells,* Chipping Campden (Glos), a set of handbells surmount and are part of the sign. There is a *Ten Bells,* and, at Trowbridge (Wilts), a *Twelve Bells.*

Rising Sun: there are many of these and most emanate from the badge of Edward III—the sun in splendour.

Seven Stars, a favourite sign in the Middle Ages, represented the seven-starred celestial crown which the Virgin Mary was usually shown wearing. Sometimes it is misconstrued and the sign shows a constellation.

Talbot: a breed of hunting dog much favoured by packmen in earlier days. Also part of the arms of the Earls of Shrewsbury.

Three Tuns derives from the Vintners' arms.

World Turned Upside Down is a whimsical sign and often represents the artist's own interpretation of the title.

D

Elephant & Castle is a popular sign still but the most famous house carrying the name was at Southwark, London, demolished a few years ago. The sign, however, still graces the new development on the site. A copper model, it was made more than fifty years ago and was a landmark dear to the hearts of Londoners. There are several theories advanced for the original naming of the tavern. One is that it was so-called from the discovery of an elephant's skeleton near London's river Fleet in 1715, but this is not very convincing and does not explain the 'castle'. Another story is that it had some connection with the trademark adopted by a brewery firm when they began to send ale to the Army in India. The emblem was, however, also the crest of the Cutlers' Company and, like so many more old trade signs, was possibly used later for an inn sign. This certainly seems a more convincing theory. The 'castle' is, of course, the howdah, the contraption used when travelling on the backs of elephants.

Cat & Fiddle is another instance of a name which has been interpreted in several ways. The generally accepted story is that it referred to a knight, Caton, who by his valour in the fighting at Calais was dubbed 'Caton le Fidele'. When an Englishman's tongue got round that it evolved as its present title. There are several versions of the sign. A cat playing a fiddle is pictured at many places, including Sowton (Devon) and the New Forest (Hants).

Goat & Compasses, several of which are still to be seen, was a popular religious sign and is believed to have been rendered down from 'God encompasses us'.

Chequers: One of the oldest signs, many of which still survive, particularly in the North of England. In medieval times it was also the emblem of the money-changer.

There are many excellent examples, including one at Chipping Norton (Oxon).

Eagle & Child, often found in the Midlands, came from the coat of arms of the Earls of Derby.

First & Last: A common sign to denote the position of the inn, first in the town—last out. At Sennen (Cornwall) the reference is to the inn's position in England.

Five Alls: a sign which always creates interest. Usually depicted are: the king who rules over all, the lawyer who pleads for all, the soldier who fights for all, John Bull who pays for all and the parson who prays for all. There are many variations. Sometimes the devil who takes all replaces one of the other figures and in country districts the farmer who, it is considered, pays for all, replaces John Bull. There are also *Four Alls* signs, such as the excellent one at Ovington (N.R. Yorks).

Signs of Trade

As early as 1512, an attempt was made at numbering the houses in a Paris street but 275 years were to pass before the system became general in France. In England, the numbering of houses and the naming of streets was enforced by a police regulation in 1805. This might well have led to a reduction in the number of signs, but by that time the public had become attached to them and fortunately they remained.

Innkeepers were by no means alone in displaying signs to advertise their calling and their wares. Most trades used signs from the fourteenth to the nineteenth centuries, particularly in the cities, and while they were never so numerous as those of the inns, many were of most attractive design. Generally, each trade carried the same type of sign. The traditional sign of the chemist, still frequently seen, was the large glass bottles known as carboys. Filled with a coloured liquid, they make an effective display. The barber's pole with its heavy red and white bands— symbolic of a gory bandage—is still a reminder that, in days gone by, the apothecary was also a surgeon. A grocer's shop was easily recognised by its three sugar-loaves and the pawnbroker by three balls, while the model of a Highlander often denoted a tobacconist.

In Creechurch Lane, London, E.C.3, the trade sign of the three sugar-loaves still hangs over a shop from which a consignment of tea was sent to America in 1773. Later jettisoned into the harbour as an act of defiance, the Boston tea party, as it became known, was one of the flash-points leading up to the outbreak of the American War of Independence.

After the Fire of London, fire insurance companies began to flourish and each had their distinctive sign which the insured person displayed on his premises.

Most cities still retain some of these trade signs but by far the greatest number of company or guild signs are perpetuated on inn signboards: carpenters', butchers' and bakers' arms are numerous, others are more rare, such as the *Plaisterers Arms*, Winchcombe (Glos).

The greatest number of signs associated with any one particular trade are those relating to the wool trade, which was for centuries the mainspring of England's prosperity. From the twelfth to the fifteenth century, in particular, England's whole economy, and indeed its politics, were built up on the trade. In the thirteenth century wool amounted to half the value of the whole land, and it has been estimated that in the fourteenth century the annual export value of the commodity amounted to seven million pounds. Much of the successful breeding of the sheep was done by the abbeys and monasteries. The signs include: *Lamb, Fleece, Golden Fleece* and *Woolpack*.

One of the most interesting sections of trade signs comprises those displayed by inns which once catered especially for a certain class of worker. In the Midlands and the North, particularly, innkeepers were apt to adopt a name, craft or process common to nearby mills or works, thereby hoping to attract those workers. The following selection is typical, and though many of the trades and crafts have long since died out, the names and signs fortunately remain. Invariably they are followed by the word 'Arms'. Those with towns noted after them are not necessarily the only ones to be found in the country:

Boltmakers, Keighley (Yorks)
Brickmakers, Halifax (Yorks)
Bricksetters, Harrogate (Yorks)
Carders, Atherton (Lancs)
Cloggers, nr Oldham (Lancs)
Cordwainers, Chorley (Lancs)
Crofters, Wigan (Lancs)
Dressers, Heywood (Lancs)
Dyers, Littleborough (Lancs)
Fellmongers, Leeds (Yorks)
Fishmongers, Wandsworth, London
Flag Cutters, nr Plymouth (Devon)
Flax Dressers, Ashby-de-la-Zouch (Leics)
Fletchers, Denton (Lancs)
Flint Knappers, Brandon (Suffolk)
Furnace, Bradford (Yorks)
Glovers, Yeovil (Som)
Graziers, Wakefield (Yorks)
Hatters, Marple (Cheshire)

Hingemakers, Ashton in Makerfield (Lancs)
Horsebreakers, Sessay (N.R. Yorks)
Hufflers (men who ferried goods from ships at anchor
to ships' chandlers establishments ashore)
Joiners, Clitheroe (Lancs)
Lathecleavers, Brighton (Sussex)
Limeburners, Billingshurst (Sussex)
Maltsters, Carlisle (Cumb)
Minders (machine minders), Oldham (Lancs)
Miners, Risehow (Cumb)
Pressers (North Country)
Printers, Blackburn (Lancs)
Ropemakers, Wigan (Lancs) and Exeter (Devon)
Sheep Shearers, Reigate (Surrey)
Slubbers, Huddersfield (Yorks) and Rochdale (Lancs)
Spindlemakers (Lancs)
Spinners, Bollington (Cheshire)
Stonemasons, Heywood (Lancs)
Thatchers, Bridgewater (Som)
Tile Sheds, Great Ayton (N.R. Yorks)
Turners, Blackburn (Lancs)
Waggonmakers, Chorley (Lancs)
Waste Dealers, Oldham (Lancs)
Welldiggers, Byworth (Sussex)
Whitesmiths (a name for a tinsmith) Gloucester and
                                              Wigan (Lancs)

The area around Totley, Sheffield (Yorks) was for long
famous for making scythes, and there is still a *Crossed
Scythes* in the village.

The *Plummer Line*, Halifax (Yorks), has associations with
the building trade, the word 'plummet' being an adaption
of the 'plumb-line' much used in the trade.

Apart from this list, which is by no means complete,
there are other names associated with local industry, the

meaning of which would only be appreciated by the 'locals'. An instance is an inn at Bulgill, Maryport (Cumb) named *Main Band*, which is a reference to a seam of coal in the Cumbrian coalfields. Another coal mining sign is the *Bonnie Pit Lad*, Hetton-le-Hole (Co. Durham).

Agricultural

IN the British Isles, where agriculture plays such an important part, there have always been a great number of signs relating to farming. Typical of these are: *Plough, Harrow, Harvest Home, Haycock, Jolly Thresher, Shepherd & Crook, Harvest Moon, Wheatsheaf* (probably the commonest in this category), *Jolly Farmer* and *Farmer's Boy. Shepherd's Boy*, Oldham (Lancs) is more unusual, as is *Cabbage* at Sefton, Liverpool. And, for good measure, there is an *Oxnoble*, Manchester, which, situated near the docks and potato wharf, is named after a species of potato.

A new approach to the same theme is the Whitbread sign of *Round of Gras*, picturing a bundle of asparagus. Badsey (Worcs) where the inn is situated, is the centre of an asparagus-growing area. A round of gras is thirty shoots; a bundle, 120 shoots.

Most counties are represented either by a 'Yeoman' with some prefix, ie *Kentish Yeoman*, or by some other country association, such as *Yorkshireman's Arms*.

The innkeeper, over the centuries, has not neglected his own calling. Starting with the *Bunch of Grapes, Vine* or *Three Tuns*, there are also represented *Malt Scoop, Malt Shovel, Leather Bottle, Bacchus, Foaming Tankard, Pewter Jug*, Lewes (Sussex), and last but by no means least, the

Jolly Brewer and *Jolly Brewmaster* of which there are numerous examples. There is also a *Jolly Topers*, Luton (Beds), *Comfortable Gill* as at Glazebury (Lancs), *Toby Jug*, near Bardon (Northumb) and *Double Barrel*, Cheltenham (Glos). Others include *Jug & Glass*, *Odd Brewers*, *Travelling Man*, Tadcaster (W.R. Yorks), and, at Picklescott (Salop), a *Bottle & Glass*.

Even cheese, which from time immemorial has been an ancillary to ale, has its share of recognition on signs: *Blue Vinny*, Puddletown (Dorset), *Cheddar Cheese*, London and Reading (Berks); *Double Gloucester*, Gloucester; *Ye Olde Cheshire Cheese*, Southampton. The word 'Stilton' appears on the sign of the *Bell Inn*, Stilton (Leics), to which farmers used to take their cheeses for sale to coach travellers.

Beast, Bird, Fish and Insect Signs

APART altogether from those which stem from heraldry, a fantastic number of signs depicting animals and birds adorn inns all over the country. The variety of poses and the colours of the animals defy all the rules of heraldry as well as Nature herself, but they are none the less picturesque and attractive.

The king of beasts, the lion, is to be found in every colour of the rainbow and many more. There are *Black Lion*, *Blue Lion*, *Brown Lion*, *Golden Lion*, *Green Lion*, *Red Lion*, *Yellow Lion* and *White Lion*. There are *Lion & Unicorn*, *Lion & Pheasant*, *Three Lions*, *Five Lions*, *Ye Olde Lion* and *Whyte Lion*.

Horses, too, not only come in all colours but are also *Rampant Horse*, *Trotting Horse*, *Flying Horse*, *Frighted*

Horse and even a *Rocking Horse*, Wakefield (Yorks). There are a *Horse & Chains*, *Horse & Crook*, *Horse* & *Trumpet*, or with its human accomplices as *Horse & Groom*, *Horse & Farrier*, and *Horse & Jockey*. There is a *Kicking Donkey*, Burwash (Sussex) and Dunmow (Essex), a *Roaring Donkey*, Holland-on-Sea (Essex) and a *Spotted Cow*, Brockham (Surrey).

The *Bear*, *Bull*, *Cow*, *Buffalo*, *Fox*, *Hare*, *Hart*, *Hind* and the humble *Mole*, abound, as might be expected, but how can we explain as English inn signs a *Gnu*, Stedham (Sussex), *Camel's Head*, Devonport (Devon), *Elephant*, *Kangaroo* (there are three in different parts of the country), *Spotted Leopard* or *Panther*, London, E.2, *Caribou*, Glasson Dock (Lancs) and *Giraffe*, Penton Place, London?

It takes the cat, however, to cut the facial capers with the *Laughing Cat* (Essex), *Squinting Cat*, *Mad Cat*, Pidley, (Hunts), *Rampant Cat*, Burford (Oxon), *Tabby Cat*, West Grinstead (Sussex) and *Ginger Tom*, Nottingham. Besides which, there are dozens of *Cat & Custard Pot*, *Cat & Fiddle* and *Old Cat*; not forgetting another kind of 'cat', with the *Polecat*, Prestwood (Bucks).

Some who specialize in the collection of bird signs claim that they total twelve to thirteen hundred and include more than sixty varieties. Certainly the list is a long one, starting with *Bird Cage*, North London, and covering wood-peckers, blackbirds, bullfinches, crows, cuckoos, doves, ducks, eagles, gulls, herons, jackdaws, owls, penguins, pheasants and scores of others down to blue tits.

At least two inns are named after the bustard, a bird the size of a turkey which became extinct in Great Britain about 1840, one of its last haunts being Salisbury Plain. One *Bustard* is in Lincolnshire, which was also a breeding-ground for the birds 100 years ago.

Fish and reptiles, too, are well represented, including such unlikely attracters of custom as crocodiles, frogs, trout and whales. New ones in this field include two Whitbread signs: the one at *Frogmill*, an old coaching house at Shipton Oliffe (Glos), shows a frog with a water mill as a background; the other, a most attractive sign at the *Lamprey*, Gloucester, depicts a lamprey encircled by a crown—lamprey pie having been a royal delicacy in medieval times. Lampreys, much sought after on the river Severn, are similar in shape to an eel but possessing no proper mouth, attach themselves to other fish in order to feed off them.

Even insects are represented in the parade by bees (sometimes even living specimens) and scorpions, while at Harlow New Town (Essex), publicans have set a delightful new trend in signs depicting butterflies. The *Painted Lady* and *Small Copper* are two particularly attractive ones and there is another very pleasing sign, the *Argus Butterfly*, at Peterlee (Co Durham).

Animals

ANTELOPE

BEAGLE

BEAR

    Bear & Bacculus
    Bear & Ragged Staff
              (Both have the same meaning)
    Bear & Bells (Beccles, Suffolk)
    Bear & Billet (Chester, Cheshire)
    Bear & Quay
    Bear & Swan
    Bear's Head

Bear's Paw
Black Bear
Brown Bear
Conquered Bear (Oldham, Lancs)
New Bear
North Pole (Clapham, London)
   (A polar bear is shown gazing up at a star)
Old Bear
Red Bear
Two Bears
White Bear

BEAVER (Ashford, Kent)

BOAR
Blue Boar
Boar's Head
Wild Boar

BUCK
Buck & Bell (Banbury, Oxon)
Buck & Dog
Buck & Hawthorn
Buck in the Park (Derby)
Buck in the Vine (Ormskirk, Lancs)
Buck's Head
Buck's Horns (Ipswich, Suffolk)
Golden Buck
Running Buck (Ipswich, Suffolk)

BUFFALO
Buffalo's Head

BULL
Black Bull
Blue Bull (Grantham, Lincs)
Bull & Butcher
Bull & Gate
Bull & Horseshoe (Harlow, Essex)

Bull & Oak
Bull & Royal
Bull & Stirrup
Bull & Swan
Bull & Wharf
Bull in Spectacles (Lichfield, Staffs)
Bull in th' Thorn
Chained Bull
Flying Bull
Golden Bull
Great Bull
Grey Bull (Haltwhistle, Northumb. and Penrith, Cumb)
Little Bull
Pied Bull (Enfield, Middx)
Red Bull
Spotted Bull (St Albans, Herts)
White Bull (Gisburn, Yorks)

CAMEL

Camel's Head (Devonport, Devon)

CAT

Cat & Custard Pot (Shipton Moyne, Wilts)
Cat & Fiddle
Cat & Lion
Cat & Mustard Pot
Cat i' t' Well (Halifax, Yorks)
Cat i' the Window
Ginger Tom
Laughing Cat
Mad Cat
Old Cat (nr Wolverhampton, Staffs)
Rampant Cat (Burford, Oxon)
Red Cat, Greasby (Cheshire)
Squinting Cat
Tabby Cat (West Grinstead, Sussex)

COW

Blue Cow (Kesteven, Lincs)
Brown Cow (common in the north)
Cow & Calf
Cow & Snuffers
Craven Heifer (this refers to the Craven Dales, Yorks.
There are several of the name in the vicinity)
Crazy Cow
Fatted Calf (Manchester, Lancs)
Heifer
Old Dun Cow
Pied Calf
Red Cow (Canvey Island, Essex)
Spotted Cow
Wensleydale Heifer (East Witton, Yorks)

DEER

Deer Leap
Red Deer

DOG

Black Dog
Chocolate Poodle (Littleton Panell, Wilts)
Claro Beagle (Harrogate, Yorks. Named after the local
Beagle Pack)
Dog & Bacon
Dog & Crook
Dog & Duck
Dog & Fox
Dog & Gun
Dog & Hedgehog (Huckley, Leics)
Dog House (Frilford, Berks)
Dog & Pheasant
Dog & Pot (Stoke Green, Bucks)
Dog & Snipe
Jack Russell (Swimbridge, Devon and Marston, Oxon)

Old Dog
Old Dog & Partridge
Pointer
Shepherd & Dog
Spotted Dog
Talbot (once a popular breed of hunting dog)
Talbot & Falcon
Twa Dogs (Keswick, Cumb)
Yorkshire Terrier

DONKEY

Donkey & Bacon
Kicking Donkey (Burwash, Sussex and Dunmow, Essex)
Roaring Donkey
Romping Donkey (Hassall Green, Cheshire)

DRAGON

Dragon's Head
Green Dragon
Red Dragon (strange to say there does not appear to be
a Black Dragon anywhere, though it figured in the arms
of Edward IV and many other prominent families)

ELEPHANT

Elephant & Castle (this was the Cutler's crest. The castle
represented the howdah, a seat on the animal's back)
Elephant & Hind (Dover, Kent)
Elephant's Head (Clapton, London)
Elephant's Nest (Tavistock, Devon)

EWE & LAMB

FOX

Fox & Burrow
Fox & Cubs
Fox & Duck
Fox & Elm
Fox & Goose
Fox & Grapes

Fox & Hounds
Fox & House
Fox & Pheasant
Fox & Rabbit
Fox's Brush (Grantham, Lincs)
Intrepid Fox (Soho, London)
Snooty Fox (Tetbury, Glos)

GOAT

Goat & Compasses
Goat's Gate
Goat's Head
Grey Goat
Royal Goat

GREYHOUND

Three Greyhounds (Bridgwater, Som. and Soho, London)

GRIFFIN

Golden Griffin (Herts)

HARE

Bell & Hare
Hare & Greyhound
Hare & Hounds
Hare's Nest

HART

Golden Hart
Hart's Head
Hart's Horns (Knaresborough, Yorks)
Red Hart
White Hart

HIND

Bald Hind
Hind's Head

HORSE

Aratan Horse (Aberford, Yorks)

Bay Horse
Black Horse
Black Horse & Harrow (Catford, London)
Bleeding Horse
Blue Horse (Great Pinton, Lincs)
Boat & Horses
Brown Horse (Neston Wirral, Cheshire and Winster, Derbys)
Dun Horse (Kendal, Westm)
Flying horse
Frighted Horse
Golden Horse
Great White Horse
Grey Horse
Grey Mare
Horse & Chains
Horse & Crook
Horse & Farrier
Horse & Groom
Horse & Jockey
Horse & Tiger (Rotherham, Yorks)
Horse & Trumpet
Kentish Horse
Little White Horse
Mare & Colt
Nag's Head
Packhorse
Pied Horse
Racehorse
Racehorses
Rampant Horse (Needham Market, Suffolk)
Red Horse
Red Horses
Rocking Horses (Wakefield, Yorks)
Royal White Horse

Page 71: (*top left*) the impressive and eye-catching sign of the *Cavalier* Grindon (Staffs); (*top right*) An unusual sign for an inn, Catforth (Lancs); (*bottom left*) Right up to date is the *Full Moon* at Taunton (Somerset); (*bottom right*) Ruthin (Denbighshire)

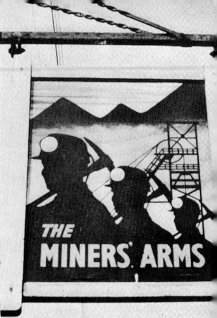

Page 72: (*top left*) Recalling an historical occasion, Maryport (Cumberland); (*top right*) This sign at Risehow (Cumberland) is, as all signs should be, self explanatory; (*centre*) Stretton (Cumberland); (*bottom*) A variation of a most popular sign at Ovington (N.R. Yorks)

Running Horses (Mickleham, Surrey)
Running Mare (Cobham, Surrey)
Sorrel Mare (Ipswich, Suffolk)
Spotted Horse (Derbys)
Suffolk Punch (Ipswich, Suffolk)
Three Colts
Trotting Mare (Overton, Hants)
Trotting Horse
White Horse
White Mare
Yorkshire Grey

HYENA (Kendal, Westm)

JAGUAR (Stourbridge, Worcs)

KANGAROO

LAMB
    Lamb & Flag
    Lamb & Lark (Oldham, Lancs)

LEOPARD
    Spotted Leopard

LION
    Black Lion
    Blue Lion
    Brown Lion
    Five Lions
    Golden Lion
    Green Lion (Rochester, Kent)
    Lion & Bell
    Lion & Fiddle
    Lion & Lamb
    Lion & Pheasant
    Lion & Snake (Lincoln)
    Lion & Swan
    Lion & Unicorn

E

Little White Lion (Cobham, Kent)
Red Lion
Red Lyon
Royal Lion
Three Lions
White Lion
Whyte Lyon (Hartley Wintney, Hants)
Ye Olde Lion
Yellow Lion

MOLE

Mole Trap (Moreton, Essex)
Three Moles

MONKEY

Blue Monkey (Plymouth, Devon)
Drum & Monkey (Brownlow, Salop)

MOUSETRAP (Bourton-on-the-Water, Glos)

NOAH'S ARK

OTTER

OX

Black Ox
Blackwell Ox
Durham Ox
Fat Ox
Grey Ox
Ketton Ox (Yarm, Durham)
Ox & Garland
Spotted Ox

PANTHER (London, E.2)

PIG

Blue Pig (Audenshaw, Lancs)
Hampshire Hog
Hog & Donkey (nr Wingham, Kent)
Little Pig (Stourbridge, Worcs)

Pig & Whistle
Sow & Pigs (Ware, Herts)
Whistling Pig

POLECAT (Prestwood, Bucks)

PONY
Welsh Pony

PORCUPINE

RABBIT
Black Rabbit
Coney (nr Wickham, Kent)
Three Rabbits (Manor Park, London)

RAM
Blue Ram (Grantham, Lincs)
Ram & Teazle
Ram's Head

RAT
Rat's Castle

REINDEER

ROEBUCK

SHEEP
Sheep's Head (Edinburgh)

SQUIRREL
Red Squirrel (Slough, Bucks)

STAG
Bald Faced Stag
Stag & Hounds
Stag & Pheasant (Macclesfield, Cheshire)
Stag's Head
Three Stags' Heads
White Stag

TIGER
Golden Tiger

Tiger's Head

UNICORN

WOLF (Norwood, London)
Bleeding Wolf (nr Sale, Cheshire)

Birds

IN heraldry, the eagle takes premier place among the birds, as does the lion among animals, and is therefore prominently featured on inn signs deriving from coats of arms, followed by other birds of prey such as the falcon, sparrow-hawk, and kite. Perhaps even more numerous, however, are signs depicting another section of birds headed by the swan—an emblem of the Vintners' Company—and including the cygnet, heron and kingfisher.

The following list of 'bird' signs is representative but by no means complete:

BIRD CAGE (North London)

BIRD IN HAND

BIRD I' T' HAND

BLACKBIRD
    White Blackbird (Loudwater, Bucks)

BLUE TIT (Broughton, Notts)

BULLFINCH (Bustard Spreyton, and in Lincs)

CHICKEN
    Black Cock
    Buff Orpington
    Cock

Cock & Blackbirds (Sudbury, Suffolk)
Cock & Bottle
Cock & Dolphin
Cock & Lion
Cock Crow
Crowing Cock (Slapton, Devon)
Fighting Cocks
Gamecock (Cheltenham, Glos)
Golden Cock
Golden Cockerel
Hen & Chickens (Hedingham, Essex)
New Cock (Hildenborough, Kent)
Three Cocks (Tetbury, Glos)
Travelling Hen (Ponts Hill, nr Ross-on-Wye, Herefs)
Ye Olde Cock

CHOUGH
Three Choughs

CRANE (Putney, London)
Three Cranes (York)

CROW (Tenbury, Worcs)
Carrion Crow (Oldham, Lancs)
Crow's Nest (Cymbran, Monmouths)

CUCKOO (Peterborough, Northants)
Cuckoo Bush (Kegworth, Leics)

DOVE
Two Doves (Bromley, Kent)

DUCK
Drunken Duck (Hawkshead, Lancs)
Ugly Duckling (Hayward's Heath, Sussex)
Wild Duck

DUTCH BIRDS (Oldham, Lancs)

EAGLE
American Eagle (Bristol)

Black Eagle (Kent)
Eagle & Child
Eagle & Hind (Chelmsford, Essex)
Eaglet
Golden Eagle
Grey Eagle (East London)
Mountain Eagle (Queensbury, Yorks)
Spread Eagle

FALCON

GOOSE

Gaping Goose
Goose & Gander
Grey Goose
Wild Goose (Combeinteignhead, Devon)

GREBE

GROUSE

GULL (nr Norwich)

HAWK

Hawk & Buck (St Helens, Lancs)
Hawk & Duck
Hawk & Partridge (Bloxham, Oxon)

HERON

JACKDAW

KINGFISHER (Cockermouth, Cumb)

KITE'S NEST (Stretton Sugwas, Herefs)

LARK (depicted on 'Rising Sun' sign, Eltham, London)

MAGPIE

Gun & Magpie (Enfield, Middx)
Magpie & Crown (Brentford, Middx)
Magpie & Stump
Three Magpies

MARTIN'S NEST (Brighouse, Yorks)

MOORCOCK
   Three Moorhens

NIGHTINGALE (Lincoln)

OSTRICH (Colnbrook, Bucks)

OWL
   Blinking Owl
   Three Owls
   White Owl

PARROT (Shelton, Beds)

PARTRIDGE

PEACOCK (Huddersfield)

PEAHEN (St Albans, Herts)

PEEWIT (Stotfold, Beds)

PELICAN

PENGUIN

PHEASANT
   Golden Pheasant (Biggleswade, Beds)

PHOENIX (mythical bird)

PIGEON
   Blue Pigeons (nr Deal, Kent)
   Pigeon Pie
   Three Pigeons

RAVEN
   Black Raven

REDWING (Lympstone, Devon)

ROBIN
   Cock Robin
   Rock Robin

ROOK

ROOKERY

SEAGULL (nr Hartlepool, Co. Durham)

SKYLARK

SNIPE

SPARROW

  Sparrow Hawk

STARLING

STORK

  Stork's Nest

SWALLOW

  Swallows

SWAN

  Black Swan
  Cygnet
  Swan & Chough
  Swan & Pyramids (North Finchley, London)
  Swan & Salmon (Derbys)
  Swan & Sugarloaf
  Swan & Talbot
  Swan with Two Necks
  Swan with Two Nicks
  Swan's Nest
  Three Swans
  White Swan

THRUSH (Bury, Lancs)
  Throstle's Nest (Wigton, Cumb and others)

TURKEY
  Turkey Cock (Norwich, Norfolk)

WOODCOCK

WOODPECKER (Leeds, Yorks)

Fish, Mammals and Reptiles

FISH were regarded with favour for coats of arms in the Middle Ages, due largely to the belief that fish were the first living things created by God. They are, therefore, quite numerous on signs, as the following list shows:

CRAB (Shoreham, Sussex)
  Crab & Lobster
  Crab Shell (Kingsbridge, Devon)

CROCODILE

DOLPHIN

FISH
  Fish & Duck
  Fish & Quart (Kegworth, Derbys)
  Fishes
  Flying Fish (Denton, nr Newhaven, Sussex)
  Laughing Fish
  Three Fishes

FROG HALL
  Three Frogs (Wokingham, Berks)
  Frogmill (Shipton Oliffe, Glos)

LAMPREY (Gloucester)

MUSSEL (Down Thomas, Devon)

PICKEREL (Beccles, Suffolk)
  Three Pickerels

PIKE & EEL (Overcote Ferry, Hunts)

PILCHARD (Bigbury, Devon)
  Pilchards (Burgh Island, Devon)
  Three Pilchards

SALMON
  Salmon Tail (Stratford on Avon, Warw)

Three Salmon

SEA HORSE (Yorks and London)

SEA SERPENT

SHRIMP

Shrimp & Turtle (Sandwich, Kent)

SNAKE

SWORDFISH (Newlyn, Cornwall—one side the fish, the other a Swordfish aircraft)

TROUT

Sea Trout (Staverton, Devon)

VIPER (Fryerning, Essex)

WHALE

Insects

BEE

Invariably the sign of the *Beehive* has some wording—a verse or line to accompany it. The eighteenth-century *Beehive* (Penrith, Cumb) has the verse:

> In this hive we are all alive
> Good liquor makes us funny,
> If you be dry step in and try
> The virtue of our honey.

The sign of the *Beehive* (Cheltenham, Glos) is surmounted with 'By industry we live'.

Bees in the Wall (Whittlesford, Cambs)

Queen Bee (East Peckham, London)

BUTTERFLIES

Argus (Peterlee, Co. Durham)

Essex Skipper
Golden Butterfly
Painted Lady (Harlow New Town, Essex)
Small Copper (Harlow New Town, Essex)

DUMB FLEA (Meldreth, Cambs)

ESSEX SERPENT

FLEA & BLANKET (nr Plymouth, Devon)

GRASSHOPPER (Westerham, Kent)

MAYFLY

SCORPION (Callington, Cornwall)

Trees, Flowers and Fruit

IT is understandable that there should be numerous inns
bearing the name of a tree, for many in days gone by,
if not now, had a tree outside the door, which naturally
became the sign. Inns named after trees and plants include:

Acorn	Holly
Alder	Juniper Berry
Apple	Lily
Bay	Lime
Beech	Mulberry
Birch	Myrtle
Cherry	Oak
Chestnut	One Elm (Stratford-upon-
Cob	Avon, Warws)
Crab Apple	Orange
Elm	Palm
Fig	Peach

Pear	White Thorn
Poplar	Willow
Sycamore	Withy
Thorn	Yew
Vine	and the Big Tree
Walnut	

Among flowers, the rose does particularly well with a variety of signs including:

English Rose (Bristol)
Rose & Thistle
Rosebud (Church, Lancs)
Rose in Bloom (Whitstable, Kent)
Rose of England
Rose Revived
Little Rose (Cambridge)

At Tonbridge (Kent) is a *Primrose* and at Ipswich (Suffolk) a *Water Lily*.

Fruit is represented by *Bunch of Cherries, Bunch of Grapes, Beauty of Bath,* and there are at least three *Pineapples,* one each at Halifax (Yorks), Bolton (Lancs) and Rochdale (Lancs).

PART THREE

Signs of Sport

NOT surprisingly, the Englishman's love of sport is well represented on signs. Here is a selection, many of which are relatively new.

FOOTBALL

Ball & Boot, Wigan (Lancs) is situated next to the ground of the Wigan Rugby League Football Club.

The Trotters, Bolton (Lancs) is named after the nickname of the Bolton Wanderers Football Club.

The Hammers, London, E.11, is another nickname. It is situated near the ground of the West Ham Football Club.

Spurs, Tottenham, London, after the football team.

Footballers Arms, Oldham (Lancs).

Next to the Rugby ground at Hartlepool (Co. Durham) is the *Touch Down*.

HORSE RACING

The achievements of many great racehorses have been commemorated by signs, particularly in the North Country:

Little Wonder, Harrogate and York.

Flying Childers, Stanton (Derbys)

Odd Spot, nr Nottingham

Charles XII, Heslington (E.R. Yorks)

Alice Hawthorne, Wheldrake (Yorks)

Altisdora, Bishop Burton (Yorks)

Windsor Lad, Windsor (Berks)

The *Cadland* situated at Old Village, Chilwell (Notts) is named after a racehorse owned by the Duke of Rutland. In 1828, it won the Derby (see below) and also the Two Thousand Guineas.

The *Running Horses*, Mickleham (Surrey) records the dead-heat which occurred in the Derby of 1828. 'Cadland' referred to above and 'The Colonel' are shown on respective sides of the signboard. The race was re-run and 'Cadland' is shown winning by a neck.

The *Smoker*, Manchester/Chester Road (Cheshire) perpetuates the name and record of a white charger owned by Lord de Tabley, who raised the Cheshire Yeomanry during the threatened Napoleonic invasion. 'Smoker' had been bred as a racehorse by the Prince Regent. Certainly it must have been a great horse, for it ran in nineteen races and won twelve of them in the period 1790-3.

The sport of kings has many other signs, including *Starting Gate, Chase, Jockey*, etc. One of the most recent is a portrait of Sir Gordon Richards at *The Champion*, Well Street, London. Gordon Richards was over twenty times champion jockey and retired in 1954.

CRICKET

There must be scores of *Cricketer's Arms* and many which are rare, such as *Full Pitcher*, Ledbury (Herefs) and *Royal Cricketers*, Old Ford, London.

HUNTING AND FISHING

Foxhunting has hundreds of signs associated with it, *Tally Ho* probably leading the field. Angling, too, has its full share, with many *Angler's Retreat* and *Fisherman*. Fish are equally well represented with *Trout, Three Fishes, Fish & Quart, Lamprey*, etc. (See also page 81.)

BOXING AND ARCHERY

Boxing has its niche with the *Noble Art*, Hampstead, London, which has its own gymnasium where Cassius Clay trained for his world championship title fight with Henry Cooper. Archery is represented by the *Long Bow*, Tunbridge Wells (Kent), where the sign shows an archer in Lincoln green, and the *Hurdler*, Stamford (Lincs) portrays another sportsman, Lord Burghley, as he then was.

The World of Literature

No one did more to popularise, indeed glamourise the English inn than Charles Dickens, who mentioned by name or inference scores of them, most of which are still with us. In recent years, an attempt has been made to have the *Great White Horse*, the 400-year old inn at Ipswich (Suffolk) demolished, but happily permission was refused. It was at this hostelry that Mr Pickwick got lost in the winding corridors and strayed into a lady's bedroom.

The *George*, Amesbury (Wilts) was the *Blue Dragon* of 'Martin Chuzzlewit'; the *King's Head*, Chigwell (Essex) was the *Maypole* of 'Barnaby Rudge'. At the *Leather Bottle*, Cobham (Kent), Pickwick discovered the lovelorn Tracy Tupman drowning his sorrows. The *Royal Hop Pole*, Tewkesbury (Glos) and the *Boot*, Grays Inn Road, London, are others identifiable with those that Dickens described. The *Crispin & Crispianus*, Rochester (Kent) is immortalised in 'The Uncommercial Traveller'. The *Grapes*, Limehouse, was the original 'Six Jolly Fellowship Porters' of 'Our Mutual Friend'. Strange to say, Dickens, himself, does not

seem to have lent his name to any inn, though Pickwick
has several and there is *Our Mutual Friend* at Stevenage
(Herts). The *George & Vulture*, Castle Court, London, is the
present meeting place of the Pickwick Club.

Many other great writers and poets appear on signs,
though only a few are duplicated. *Shakespeare, Burns,
Scott, Tennyson* and *Keats* (both of the latter on the Isle
of Wight), *Byron, Macaulay, Wordsworth* are among those
honoured, as is *Samuel Pepys*, the diarist, at Gillingham
(Kent), and *John Evelyn*, at Deptford (Wilts).

Less famous perhaps is John Collier, who was the son
of a curate at Stretford (Lancs). He became well known as
a Lancashire dialect poet, writing under the pseudonym
of '*Tim Bobbin*', the name of the inn which perpetuates
his memory at Rochdale (Lancs). There is a *Dr Syntax*, Oldham (Lancs) named after the works of William Combe.

Favourite characters in many books feature as names of
inns and most of them have appropriate signs. These include *Peveril of the Peak, Bailie Nicol Jarvie, Lady of the
Lake* (Sir Walter Scott). The *Gordon Arms*, nr St Mary's
Loch (Pebbleshire) carries a plaque which states that there
Sir Walter Scott in the autumn of 1830 met the Ettrick
shepherd and parted for the last time. *Moon & Sixpence*
(Somerset Maugham) and *Endymion* (Keats) are other names
associated with famous authors and poets.

It would seem that many of the great story writers of
the past did much of their work in the inns of England.
Daniel Defoe, it is claimed, wrote part of 'Robinson
Crusoe' at the *Old Cock*, Halifax (Yorks), part at the
Llandoger Trow, Bristol, and is reputed to have met the
original Crusoe, Alexander Selkirk, at the *Black Dog*, Wey-
mouth (Dorset). At the village of Denton, nr Canterbury
(Kent), the Rev H. Barham, who wrote under the pen
name of Thomas Ingoldsby, lived for a time and the inn
bears the name of *Jackdaw* in consequence. Similarly the

Page 89: (*top left*) Quite unique is the *No Tick* at Leeds; (*top right*) An attractive 'George' at Guildford (Surrey); (*bottom left*) An appropriate sign for Grimsby; (*bottom right*) Another such, Longney (Glos)

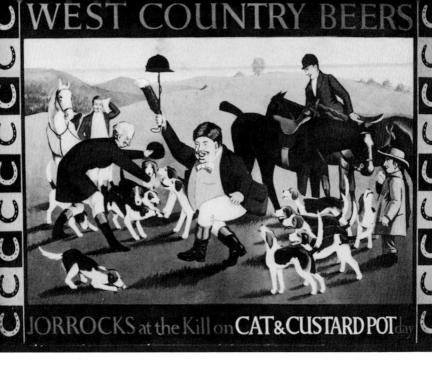

Page 90: (top) A humorous sign in the 'literary' section at Shipton Moyne (Wilts); (bottom) One of the few remaining 'beam' or 'gallows' signs at Stoneham (Suffolk)

Jolly Farmer, Farnham (Surrey), recalls that William Cobbet was born in the village in 1762. In Shipton Moyne (Wilts) there is a *Cat & Custard Pot*, which reminds the passer-by of R. S. Surtees' famous novel 'Handley Cross'. There is a *John Jorrocks* at Frittenden (Kent), Russell Thorndike in his 'Dr Syn' novels drew on two inns, *The Ship* and *City of London*, Dymchurch (Kent), and Jeffery Farnol used the *Bull*, Sissinghurst (Kent) in his book 'The Broad Highway'.

Conan Doyle's most famous character is perpetuated at the *Sherlock Holmes*, Charing Cross, London, where an autograph book kept by the manager bears signatures of visitors from over fifty different countries, including a number behind the Iron Curtain.

Two inns at Bristol claim to be the original *Spyglass* of Robert Louis Stevenson's 'Treasure Island'. They are the *Llandoger Trow* and the *Hole in the Wall*. There is no real evidence for either but both must have been at the centre of the slave trade, press-gang and pirate activities of their day. It is claimed also that Mary Read, the woman pirate, frequented these Bristol taverns.

A sixteenth-century inn at Ringmore (Devon) was for long the haunt of smugglers and R. C. Sherriff spent some time there while working on his famous play, 'Journey's End', after the First World War. To commemorate the association, the name of the inn was changed to *Journey's End*.

Fairy story heroes and heroines have also achieved lasting fame on signs. There is the *Pied Piper* at St Leonards (Sussex), *Mother Hubbard* at Loughton (Essex), *Jack & Jill* Coulsdon (Surrey) and Stockport (Cheshire), *Robin Hood* at Beacontree (Essex) and his jovial henchman, *Little John*, at York. At Northampton, there is the *Marquis of Carabas*, taken from 'Puss in Boots', and Batley (Yorks) has the *Babes in the Wood*.

F

Historical and Martial Signs

WITH Britain's long tradition of military service it was inevitable that there should be a wealth of signs recalling past wars and famous victories, as well as a fair quota remembering the men who served in them. Some of the generals and officers have already been mentioned, though often the reason for their being so commemorated is obscure. Signs to the ordinary soldier are more understandable and reflect centuries of British military history. They range from signs of the *Fencibles, Volunteer,* and names of famous regiments which have served down the years to the Home Guard of the last war.

Included among them are such names as: *Artilleryman, Rifleman, Fusilier, Grenadier, Recruiting Sergeant, Light Dragoon, Light Horseman, Scots Greys, Royal Lancer, Royal Dragoon* and—a very new one—the *Trumpet Major,* nr Dorchester (Dorset). There are *Troopers, Loyal Troopers, Old Sergeant,* Enfield (Middx), *Vigilant Soldier, Drummer* and, of course, *Gun* and *Cannon,* while almost every county has a sign commemorating its own Volunteers or Yeomanry.

Another new sign, and a particularly attractive one, is the *Old Comrade,* Wellington (Herefs) which shows an 'Old Comrade' complete with bowler hat and row of medals, typical of men we have been accustomed to see at British Legion services over the years. The licensee of the inn is himself an 'Old Comrade' of the Herefordshire Light Infantry. Also right up-to-date is the *Red Beret,* Chelmsford (Essex) and the *Desert Rat,* Reigate (Surrey).

Wars and battles are perpetuated by signs which include *Crimea,* Castleford (Yorks), and some of its battles: *Balaclava, Alma, Inkerman, Sebastapol.* There are others of *Waterloo, Malta, Gibraltar Castle, Cyprus, Cuba* and scores

more which reflect past triumphs all over the globe. Rare
are *Cape of Good Hope*, Goole (Yorks) and the now almost
forgotten battles of the Sikh war, such as *Moodkee*, Malvern (Worc). There is also a *Blenheim*, and a *Minden Rose*,
Bury St Edmunds (Suffolk), its sign depicting a rose sur-
mounting a file of tricorn-hatted redcoats, men of the 12th
Foot Regiment who fought with such distinction at the
battle of Minden in 1759. Near the Castle, Edinburgh, is
the *Ensign Ewart*, which commemorates Ewart of the Scots
Greys, who captured one of Napoleon's standards at the
battle of Waterloo. Another splendid sign, ten feet high,
is that of the *Cavalier*, Grindon (Staffs), with its painting
of a cavalier mounted on a rearing horse.

Surprisingly the Navy lags behind the Army in numbers
of inn sign associations. There are a few, such as *British
Tar* and *Royal Marine* and quite a number of *Sailor Boy*
and *Jolly Tar*. Few naval engagements are commemorated
but ships and their figureheads show up a little better.
One of the earliest is the *Golden Hind*, Musbury (Devon)
and Plymouth (Devon), and there is a *Trafalgar Bay* at
York. At most seaports, too, there are signs with some
sort of association with the Navy and seafarers, such as
The Navy, Mariner, Dolphin, etc.

Great Events

MANY inns named during the last few years have associated
themselves with events or incidents of the last two great
wars. At Gravesend (Kent) there is a *Battle of Britain*, a *Dover
Patrol* at Blackheath, London, a *Parachute* at Henlow (Beds)
and a *Happy Landing* at Stanwell (Middx). *The Guinea Pig*,

East Grinstead (Sussex), was named in commemoration of the Guinea Pig Club, an association of 600 airmen of fourteen different nationalities who were badly burned in the last war and treated by plastic surgery at the famous hospital nearby. The sign bears the club's badge—a guinea pig in a Spitfire descending in flames.

The Military Tournament held annually at Olympia, London, now has a *Tournament*, nr Earls Court, as a permanent reminder of the event.

The *Beacon, Bromley* (Kent) recalls the fire beacons which were once set up round the coast to warn of national dangers or at times of rejoicing.

Another type of beacon is the *Belisha Beacon*, Gillingham (Kent), a reminder that this now familiar feature of our roads—named after a Minister of Transport, Leslie Hore Belisha—came into use quite a long while ago.

London Airport has its *Air Hostess*, and the *Man of Steel*, Pontfaen, Newport (Mon) refers to the workers of the most modern steel plant of its kind in Europe, which is close by.

The Severn Bridge & Railway is the name of the inn at Sharpness (Glos) and the very fine sign shows the bridge which once spanned the nearby river.

At Bushey (Herts) is the *Leefe Robinson*, commemorating Captain W. L. Robinson who was awarded the Victoria Cross for shooting down the first Zeppelin at Cuffley (Herts) in 1916.

▰▰▰▰▰▰▰▰▰▰

Through the centuries, notable events as well as illustrious people have inspired enterprising licensees in their choice of names for their inns. The list is long and varied, and the following is only a small selection :

Hadrian's Wall, Hexham (Northumb).

Martello, Folkestone (Kent) is a reminder of the towers which were built off the south coast at the time of the Napoleonic invasion scare, in much the same way as tank traps and pill-boxes were erected to repel the Germans had they made the attempt in 1939.

Free Trade, Wigan (Lancs) and Leicester.

Drake's famous game of bowls on Plymouth Hoe illustrates the sign of the *Plymouth*, Bridport (Dorset).

The legion of *Royal Oak* signs usually refer to Charles II's escape after the battle of Worcester. Some have perpetuated other events. The *Royal Oak*, Shoreham (Kent), has a sign of the battleship of that name. The board of the *Royal Oak*, Newingreen (Kent), reproduces the medal issued to commemorate the restoration of the monarchy. On the Royal Mile, Edinburgh, is the *Covenanter*, which stands hard by Covenanter's Close and but a few yards from St Giles Cathedral. Here, in 1637, the famous Jemmy Geddes riot took place, when an attempt was made to introduce the new prayer book.

It was a great national tragedy when the 'Royal George', flagship of Admiral Kemenfelt, sank suddenly in Portsmouth harbour on August 29, 1782. It is remembered by a sign on the *Royal George*, Lionsholl (Yorks).

The *Bounty*, Maryport (Cumb) recalls the famous mutiny of 1789. The interest is local in that Fletcher Christian, leader of the mutineers, was born close by.

The ceiling of the lounge of the *Discovery*, Cardiff, represents Antartica, the inn having been named after the ship of Captain Scott, the famous explorer.

Live & Let Live, as the name of an inn, is often to be found in the North Country. They came by the name after the 'Hungry Forties'.

The *Union* is quite a popular sign still and referred to the union of England and Scotland in 1707. Their number was augmented in 1801 when the union of Great Britain and Ireland became effective.

In the year 1314, as every Scotsman knows, Robert the Bruce defeated the army of Edward II. Close to the site of the battlefield today is an inn, bearing the succinct name *1314*.

The Great Exhibition of 1851 is commemorated by several signs including the *Crystal Palace*, St Albans (Herts) and Tunbridge Wells (Kent), also the *Glass House*, Old Swan, Liverpool.

The *Grand Trunk*, Birkenhead (Cheshire) similarly commemorates the building of the Leeds-Liverpool canal, which was opened in 1816. Due largely to financial difficulties, it took forty-six years to complete the 127 miles and cost £1,200,000.

It is fitting that at least one inn is named after the great steamship built by Isambard Brunel in 1858. This iron ship, which began with such high hopes, had a fantastic life. She was used to lay the Atlantic cable, caused thirteen lawsuits, was put up for auction six times and ended as a floating circus. Her name is remembered by the *Great Eastern*, New Ferry, Wirral (Cheshire).

Mixed-up and Humorous Signs

SOME inns have names which defy all reason and seem to have been dreamed up by someone who had imbibed too freely. Yet there is usually some reason even for the most apparently absurd. Sometimes it is because a mistake has been perpetuated over the years—even the centuries—and perhaps the best example of this is the sign of the *Black Prince*. Originally it honoured the warrior son of Edward III, probably named soon after his victory at Crecy. In time, the elements played havoc with the colours and the sign practically faded out. An artist with little knowledge of history repainted it strictly according to its title, with the final result of an Indian chief sporting feathers in a headband.

Mis-spelling accounts for the *Frighted Horse*—the animal carrying a packman's wares was, of course, the 'freighted' horse—and there are numerous examples of inn names formed by odd combinations of words. The *Swan & Railway, Railway & Linnet, Beehive & Cross Keys*, Leeds (Yorks) are typical, and examples from the animal world include *Elephant & Hind*, Dover (Kent) and *Horse & Tiger*, Rotherham (Yorks). Some are undoubtedly a combination of what were formerly two different inns. Perhaps one establishment falling on difficult times was amalgamated with another, and the surviving licensee retained both names in the hope of doubling his custom.

The British sense of humour was bound to find an outlet in inn signs and the many witty ones in this category help to compensate for some of the more hackneyed ones.

Angel, Ware (Herts) is not quite what one would expect for the sign shows a boy who has just loosed his catapult, looking at the damage he has inflicted on a window. Another amusing sign is the *No Tick*, Leeds (Yorks), which shows a clock face.

A 'snig' is a Lancashire word for an eel, and *The Snig's Foot*, Ormskirk (Lancs) deserves a place in this section since an eel, of course, has no feet. At Nailsworth (Glos) the *Weighbridge*, has a sign depicting an enormous bridge, with a woman of equally generous proportions on it.

Many inns have names which are brief and to the point, as *Nog Inn*, *Nobody Inn*, *Who'd have thought it*, *Listen Inn*, *No Hurry*, *Never Inn*, *Why Not*, *Drop Inn*, Guisley (Yorks), *Wanted Inn*, Sparrowpit, nr Buxton(Derbys), *Slow & Easy*, Lostock Graham (Cheshire) and *Young Vanish Inn*, Mansfield-Chesterfield Road (Notts/Derbys),

Famous are *Quiet Woman*, *Good Woman* or *Headless Woman*, the signs all showing a woman without a head. The *Quiet Woman*, Earl Sterndale (Derbys), has an inscription over the picture 'Soft words turneth away wrath'. In the same category is the *Honest Lawyer*, Kings Lynn (Norfolk), which shows a lawyer holding his head on his hand and, with main-line terminus stations particularly in mind, the *Jolly Porter* should perhaps be included in this humorous section.

Everyday Expressions which Stem from Inns

QUITE a number of expressions now common in our language have originated from inns, or are associated with famous characters depicted on inn signs. Here are some of them:

'All Sir Garnet' came to be accepted as signifying that everything was in good order and there was nothing to worry about. This arose from the public's regard and faith in that great soldier, Sir Garnet Wolseley, who was eminently successful in most of his campaigns, which included the Burmese war, the Indian Mutiny, Canada and the Sudan. The *Garnet Wolseley* in the market place at Norwich is named in his honour.

In the coaching era there were two inns at Stony Stratford (Bucks), the *Cock* and the *Bull*, and between them a fierce rivalry existed. As the coaches arrived from different directions, the gossip of the road was exchanged, and lost nothing in the telling. So much so that anything which resembled a gross exaggeration or was obviously distorted became known as a 'Cock and Bull story', a saying still in use all over the country.

The *Eagle Tavern*, City Road, London, was situated in an area much frequented by tailors, and one of the tools of their trade was a type of iron known as a 'weazel'. Their all too frequent visits to the tavern obliged many of them to visit the pawnshop before pay day to 'pop' their weazel, from which came the jingle:

> Up and down the City Road
> In and out the Eagle
> That's the way the money goes.
> 'Pop goes the weazel'.

Mr Brock, founder of the famous firework manufacturers, had a large family and when he suffered catastrophe as the result of an explosion, he was all but bankrupt. By the generosity of the owner of the *Eagle Tavern*, he was allowed to hold a Benefit Night in the then spacious garden of the inn and it was so successful that it put him back on his feet financially. 'Brock's Benefit' thereafter referred to something lucky or gratuitous.

At Warwick there is an inn called *Hobson's Choice*, a name it has borne since the seventeenth century when an innkeeper, Tobias Hobson, used to hire out horses. No matter the preferences of his customers, he was adamant that the animals should be used in strict rotation, so that anyone requiring a horse had to take the one selected by Hobson, or none at all—thus when there is no choice in the matter it is 'Hobson's choice'.

The Marquis of Granby, a distinguished soldier who took part in the Seven Year's War, was among other things a brilliant cavalry leader. As Colonel of the Blues, he led a charge at the battle of Warburg and in the turmoil and excitement his wig blew off. As he galloped ahead of his troops the sun shone on his bald pate, and he so inspired his men that they afterwards boasted how the Marquis 'went for the enemy bald-headed', an expression that has ever since meant to undertake an enterprise with vigour.

The phrase 'to peg away' is believed to have come from the use of the peg tankard, which in former days held two quarts of ale. It was marked with eight pins at equal distances to allow half-a-pint from one pin to the next. Some were apt to drink more than their share, hence the phrase 'to pull someone down a peg'.

And not only English usage! The tune of the American national anthem, the 'Star Spangled Banner', originated at the *Crown & Anchor Tavern*, Arundel Street, Strand, London, where it began as an English song. In the 1790s the Anacreontic Society used to meet at the inn for concerts of songs or orchestral music. The song which was later adapted by the Americans was originally John Stafford Smith's 'To Anacreon in Heaven', which always ended the group's proceedings. The Society took its name from the Greek lyric poet who lived *circa* 500 years BC and who wrote chiefly in praise of love and wine.

Not What They Seem

THE *Last Inn*, Barmouth (Merion), does not mean what it implies, for the sign shows a rasp being used on a shoe which is on a last.

The sign of the *Cat & Cracker*, Grain (Kent), shows a cat being startled by a cracker, but, in fact, the name is derived from a catalytic cracker at the nearby oil refinery.

When the local railway line at Fordingbridge (Hants) closed, the inn outside the station changed its name from the *Railway Tavern* to the *Load of Hay*.

A modern sign that falls into this category is the *Pilt Down* (Sussex), named after the Pilt Down man, which turned out to be a fraud.

The numerous signs of the *Union* usually commemorate the Union Acts of 1707 and 1801, but the sign of the *Union*, Leek (Staffs), shows a man and a woman of medieval times being married.

Bird in the Hand, Bagshot (Surrey), has a sign showing a Regency beau with his arm round a girl's waist, instead of the usual falcon resting on a man's wrist.

The *Chieftain* at Morecambe (Lancs) is not an Indian chief but a ship's figurehead.

At Styal (Cheshire) the *Ship Inn* has no nautical connotation but is said to have come from the northern dialect word 'shippen'—meaning cowshed.

The *Carnarvon Castle*, Oxton, Birkenhead (Cheshire), would at first sight appear to be incorrectly spelt. It however, is correct, and is the third inn of this name to occupy the site, the last one having been destroyed by enemy action.

Oldest, Highest, Smallest—

HE would be a bold man indeed who would categorically state that any one inn is the oldest in Britain. First there is the difficulty of trying to determine whether a place has been an inn continuously. Then, though experts may pronounce on the age of the buildings, most include both old parts and others which have been subject to demolition and rebuilding over the years. A great many inns have strong claims to their age, but few can substantiate them.

The *Fountain*, Canterbury (Kent) undoubtedly had prior claims but, unfortunately, it was destroyed by enemy aircraft in World War II. Its nearest successor to the title is probably the *Falstaff*, formerly the *Pilgrim's Rest*, Canterbury, believed to have been adapted as a halting place for pilgrims in 1422, when it was already old.

Others high on the list of patriarchs among inns are:

The *Angel & Royal*, Grantham (Lincs) on the Great North Road. Experts have declared some of the cellar masonry to be dated about 1213. The building was originally owned by the Knights Templar and on its Gothic archway are carved likenesses in stone of Edward III and his queen. This inn was originally the *Angel*, the 'Royal' being added after a visit by Edward VII when Prince of Wales.

The *Ostrich*, Colnbrook (Bucks), was a hospice somewhere in the region of 800 years ago.

The *Star* is certainly of a great age, for the village of Alfriston (Sussex) in which it stands is recorded in the Domesday Book. At the time of its building the inn was a place of sanctuary.

The *Fighting Cocks*, St Albans (Herts), is built on the site of the water-gate of St Albans Abbey and, if not the oldest inn, is certainly the oldest inhabited house in the town.

The *Turk's Head*, which stands next to Exeter's ancient Guildhall, also has a very good claim, for it is mentioned in the year 1289, when the city authorities granted the proprietors the right to lean a beam against the Guildhall in consideration of a payment of one penny a year.

Ye Olde Bell, Hurley (Berks), was built originally as a guest-house to a Benedictine monastery. How long it has been an inn is not recorded.

The *White Horse*, Dorking (Surrey), dates from the thirteenth century and was formerly owned by the Knights of St John of Jerusalem.

The *George & Dragon*, Codicote (Herts), is said to have stood there since the thirteenth century, as has the *Artichoke* at Christow (Devon) and the *Chequers* at Tonbridge (Kent).

Certainly very ancient is the *Trip to Jerusalem*, Nottingham. The foundations of the building go back to 1070.

The *George & Vulture*, Lombard Street, London, is said to be of twelfth-century origin.

The *New Inn*, Gloucester, one of the few remaining galleried inns, dates from the fifteenth century, and another ancient building is the *Four Swans*, Waltham Cross (Herts).

The *George*, Norton St Philip (Som), was once a hostel used by pilgrims, and ranks high on the seniority list.

Leicester's oldest inn is the *Saracen's Head*, which stands on land granted to Leicester Abbey in 1312. The inn has been rebuilt in recent years. Another Everard house in the city is the *Mitre & Keys*. Under the inn there is a tunnel which is said to connect St Nicholas's church with the castle, though no one has explored it within living memory.

Highest

THE *Tan Hill* is almost certainly the inn with the highest position in the British Isles, for it stands on the summit of Stainmoor on the moorland road between Reeth (N.W. Yorks) and Brough (Westm), 1,732 ft above sea level. It also has one of the loneliest situations, for it is three and a half miles from the nearest telephone and five miles from the nearest village.

A runner-up for the claim of the highest is the *Cat & Fiddle*, five miles from Buxton (Derbys). It stands 1,690 ft above sea level—a mere 42 ft lower than *Tan Hill*—but claims the superiority of enjoying a seven-day licence.

The *Traveller's Rest* on the summit of the Kirkstone

Pass (Westm) is 1,500 ft up, followed by the *Warren* inn on Dartmoor (Devon) which is 1,450 ft above sea level.

Smallest

THERE is nothing like the same eagerness to claim the title of the smallest inn, but this distinction possibly goes to the *Smiths Arms*, Godmanstone (Dorset), which measures only 20 by 10 ft, the eaves of its thatched roof being only 4 ft from the ground.

A contender for the title is the *Nutshell*, Bury St Edmunds (Suffolk), where the bar measures 12 by 7 ft.

Largest

THIS title undoubtedly goes to the *Downham Tavern*, Bromley (Kent), which was opened in 1930 to serve the local housing estate. There are two bars, one 45 ft in length and another 60 ft, making it possible to serve over 1,000 customers at a time.

Longest and Shortest Names

STALYBRIDGE (Cheshire) boasts the inn carrying the longest name, *13th Mounted Cheshire Riflemen* and two which

Page 107: (*top*) An old trade sign at Winchcombe (Glos); (*bottom*) Informative and colourful is the hunting scene at Keswick (Cumberland)

Page 108 : (top) A most attractive sign at Plumley (Cheshire); (bottom) Christmas card effect at Clifton (Bristol)

tie for the shortest are the *C.B.* nr Richmond (Yorks) and the *XL*, Garstang (nr Lancaster). Another equally short name, *GI.*, meaning the American infantrymen, is no longer in being.

They Like the Old Ones Best

SINCE the days of Trafalgar, an inn at Burnham Overy, Staithe (Norfolk), had been known as *The Hero* and its sign carried a portrait of Lord Horatio Nelson, the local boy who made good. In 1963, the brewers decided to change the name to that of Wing Commander Guy Gibson, VC, who led the famous 'dam buster' raid in the last war. When the intention became known there was such an immediate local outcry that the brewers were soon persuaded to change their mind instead of the name, and so Lord Nelson remains as the local hero.

Reaction of a different kind was evoked when the traditional sign of an angel at the *Angel*, Braintree (Essex) was changed for one showing an angel holding a foaming tankard, the froth topped by a halo. Strong protests were made by the local vicar and others but the new version with the haloed beer remains.

Over 100 years ago a row of cottages at Sleaford (Lincs) was converted into an inn, named the *Buckle*. In 1963, a

G

new building which had cost £28,000, was opened to take its place and the owners, Tamplin's Brewery Ltd, proposed to rename it *The Goldfish*, in tribute to the 'Goldfish' Club, membership of which comprises RAF personnel rescued from aircraft which 'ditched' or were shot down into the sea during the last war. There was, however, such a loud outcry that the old name was retained though, oddly enough, no one seems to know how the inn came to be named the *Buckle* in the first place.

Perhaps the most surprising protest was over the naming of the *Sir Winston Churchill*, Bamford (Derbys) which was opened by Dutton's Brewery Ltd in 1965, to take the place of the *Golden Fleece* close by, scheduled for demolition. A local petition organised and presented to the brewers, stated that the *Golden Fleece* had occupied the site for 350 years and should be retained. The petition was unsuccessful.

Strange but True

FEW inns today can boast that they are inaccessible to motor-cars but this is true of the *Red Lion*, in the quaint North Devon village of Clovelly. Guests who go to stay at the inn have either to walk or be transported from the car park by Land Rover.

A car on the roof of the *Derby Arms*, Inskip (Lancs), serves as a somewhat unusual sign as well as a landmark.

At Sotheby's saleroom in May 1968, a painting 'Outside the Red Lion' was sold for £6,800. The work of William Shayer Senior, and measuring 39½ in by 51½ in, the picture shows rustics with horses, donkeys and dogs, and a roadside inn in the background.

Gargantuan beer drinkers from all over the world assembled in the Yorkshire village of Bilton, nr Hull, to hold the first world beer-drinking contest in June 1968, one of a number of events to raise money for a local project. Although 200 competitors were expected, only eight actually took part, including 40-stone 'Klondike Bill' from Alaska. The winner of the contest was spiderman Lionel Tutt, who gulped down seventeen pints of bitter in sixty minutes and then collapsed. There was also a 'yard of ale' competition, the winner of which downed a 2¾-pint yard in exactly fourteen seconds. The fastest pint award went to a man who drank it down in 3.2 seconds. *The chairman of the Events Committee was a teetotaller, and the village of Bilton does not possess an inn.*

In 1842, the villagers of Horbling, nr Sleaford (Lincs), decided that they needed an inn and raised the money to build one. Today, it still pays the locals to drink at *The Plough*, as the parish council owns the inn and the rent it receives from the brewery goes towards the relief of rates, now the lowest in the rural district. The family who run the place have done so since the council was formed in 1894.

●●●●●●●●●●●

Bracken, a donkey, is owned by Mr & Mrs Forbes, licensees of the *Lamb*, Wantage (Berks). This remarkable animal has its own mug, is an ardent Guinness drinker and is sometimes brought into the bar for a drink. He was born in Eire, which may account for his taste for Guinness.

●●●●●●●●●●●

A really delightful sign hangs outside a former inn at Hollins Moor (Cheshire) which, for centuries, was known as the *Hare & Hounds*. Some years ago, however, it was purchased by a lady as a hostel for the Girl Guide movement. Now, under its new name, *The Children's Inn*, the strongest brew is ginger beer, but it is none the less popular on that account.

●●●●●●●●●●●

During the early years of the eighteenth century, Jeremiah Carter, curate of Lastingham (Yorks), kept an alehouse as well as carrying out his parish duties. His habit was to play the fiddle while his parishioners quaffed his beer, which was enjoyable for all and also augmented his stipend.

●●●●●●●●●●●

At Bosham (W. Sussex) there is an inn—*The Anchor Bleu*—which probably received its name in an early attempt to foster the *entente cordiale*.

●●●●●●●●●●●

The Wellington boot got its name from the Duke of Wellington and, in St Albans (Herts), two inns on opposite sides of a street are called, respectively, *Wellington* and *Boot*.

On the ring road at Norwich (Norfolk) stands the *Whifflers*. The name could have come from the dictionary definition of a 'whiffler'—one who frequently changes his opinion—but more likely it refers to the word 'whiffle', a small flute or fife.

The old name of Perth (Scotland) was *St Johnstoun* and this is perpetuated by the inn of that name in the city today. It is also the title of the local football team.

A British inn was opened in 1966 at Tokyo (Japan) in the busiest part of the city.

On the anniversary of its namesake's ninety-first birthday (1965) an inn, the *Sir Winston Churchill*, was opened by the British Ambassador, near the Arc de Triomphe in Paris.

The shape of things to come? The *White Hart*, King's Road, Chelsea, London, has been renamed the *Drug Store*. In addition to the bars, there are a boutique, a chemist's shop and a delivery service run by girls on motor-cycles.

Reference has previously been made to how, in earlier times, street names were often taken from the principal inn of the district. At Birkenhead (Cheshire) the position has been reversed for the new *Avenue* inn is named after a cinema, which formerly occupied the site until it was destroyed by enemy action in 1941.

＊＊＊＊＊＊＊＊＊＊＊＊

Until recently the village of Farnborough (Hants) had no post office and people had to go two miles to the nearest. Now a post office has been opened at the *Butchers Arms* in the village.

＊＊＊＊＊＊＊＊＊＊＊＊

In the year 1849, barley was 28s a quarter. There was then an excise duty on malt and hops but none on beer. When it was imposed, the duty was 7s 9d a standard barrel. Today, the duty is in the region of £17 13s od (standard barrel of 1,055 degrees).

＊＊＊＊＊＊＊＊＊＊＊＊

There are only two areas in Britain where the inns are owned by the State and any profits from the undertakings remitted to the Treasury. In the Carlisle area the scheme has operated since 1951. There are 174 such houses in Carlisle and North Cumberland.

＊＊＊＊＊＊＊＊＊＊＊＊

Intensive research would be needed to ascertain the number of inns and taverns in particular cities at different eras. It is known, however, that in 1842 Manchester, with a population of 400,000, had 475 taverns and 1,143 beer houses—equivalent to one drinking place for each 250 head of the population!

PART FOUR

Inns with a Story

A MAN who in his lifetime was known as 'the modern Methuselah' has an inn sign to his memory—at the *Henry Jenkins*, Kirkby Malzeard (Yorks). A native of Ellerton-upon-Swale (Yorks), Jenkins claimed to have been born in 1501 and one of his early memories was of being sent to North Allerton at the age of twelve with a horseload of arrows at the time of the battle of Flodden. He was buried at Bolton-on-Swale in 1667 and an obelisk to his memory was erected in the churchyard in 1743. He certainly lived to an extraordinary age, but his claim to a span of 166 years is very much open to doubt.

The most corpulent Englishman, according to authentic records, is immortalised by a sign at Leicester, where he was born in 1770. He was Daniel Lambert, son of the keeper of Leicester jail, and soon after succeeding his father in that post his size and weight began to increase enormously. By the time he was twenty-three, he weighed thirty-two stone and began to turn his corpulence to good account. He had a special carriage built in which he travelled to London and put himself on show at a house in Piccadilly. This he continued to do with great success at various places until his sudden death in 1809, while staying at the *Waggon & Horses*, Huntingdon (Hunts). The cause of his death was fatty degeneration of the heart, and he was then 5 ft 11 in tall and weighed 52¾ stone. To make his coffin, 112 superficial feet of elm was used. A suit of his clothes is still preserved in the museum at Stamford (Lincs), and the waistcoat has a girth of 102 in. A chair made for him is on view at Peterborough Museum. Small wonder that he figures on the sign of the *Daniel Lambert*, Leicester.

Another famous character to adorn a sign is John Middleton, who was born in the Lancashire village of Hale in 1578. At an early age he was renowned for his great strength and eventually grew to a height of 9 ft 3 in. He was taken to London to fight the king's wrestler, whom he conquered so thoroughly that his welcome went cold and he was given £20 from James I to go home again. Eventually he married a fisherman's daughter and lived to the age of forty-five. Buried in the local churchyard, his grave still attracts many sightseers. At the *Childe of Hale*, Hale (Lancs), the sign carries a likeness based on a life-sized drawing which was originally at Brasenose College, Oxford. Also displayed at the inn is an outline of the giant's hand, measuring 8½ in across and 17 in from wrist to finger-tips.

The Cornish giant, Antony Payne, was born at the *Tree*, Stratton (Corn), in 1610. He was 7 ft 4 in in height and weighed thirty-eight stone. A portrait of him by Sir Godfrey Kneller is in the Royal Institute at Truro.

Another piece of local history which survives through an inn sign is the story of two famous poachers who thrived in Hertfordshire some fifty years ago. They were the sons of one, Henry Fox, who saw to it that they received a strict upbringing and went to chapel regularly. Whilst they were identical in appearance and were given the same two Christian names, there were distinct differences in their characters.

Ebenezer Albert, named after the chapel where his father was a lay preacher, was taciturn and would spend hours in a public house drinking. Albert Ebenezer, on the other hand, was a good-natured humorist and his frequent appearances at the local police-court meant a field day for all concerned. He had a set piece which he related with the air of a man making a public address, and his repartee made everyone laugh, including the magistrates. On one occasion he produced a Baptist hymn book to support his claim that he was only in the woods at midnight to polish up his hymn singing!

The fact that the twins were identical in appearance gave them a superb alibi in court, and it was impossible for those prosecuting to be certain they had the right culprit in the dock. Sometimes indeed, the wrong one was sentenced, a mistake each would take quite philosophically. After all, it worked both ways. Both men were much liked, even admired, by the locals and once when Edward VII, then Prince of Wales, was waiting in the local inn after his motor car had broken down, he appeared to be highly amused at the stories Albert had to tell.

Ebenezer died through leaving a hospital bed for one more look at the fields and covers where he had spent his life. Albert died in hospital and up to the last was visited by the local gentry, whom he called his friends notwithstanding that some of them in the past had contributed to his 120 poaching convictions.

A fine sign at the *Twin Foxes*, Stevenage New Town (Herts), shows the Fox brothers in silhouette with their guns under their arms.

An eccentric and rather pathetic figure is the subject of a sign near Ilkley (Yorks). He was Joe Job Senior who, in his youth, had been a man of many parts: farm-labourer, woolcomber, and dry waller. An additional accomplishment was his ability to sing in four voices—alto, treble, tenor and bass—and in this role he appeared at the Leeds theatre. His great fondness for drink was probably the reason why he was never in regular employment and at the age of sixty he married an eighty-year-old widow. This so annoyed her relatives that when she died they pulled down the cottage in which the couple had lived. Job thereupon built himself a hovel measuring only 3 ft by 5 ft on the edge of the moor, and lived as a hermit. He made his clothes out of sacks, wore a horse's bellyband as a belt and wrapped his legs in straw for warmth. Blocks of wood, stuffed with straw, served as shoes. He died at the age of seventy-seven, killed by drugs which some locals had mixed with his drink in an ill-conceived joke. Today, the *Hermit Inn*, Burley Woodhead, nr Ilkley (Yorks), carries a sign which keeps alive the memory of this unfortunate man.

At Stretton (Rutland) on the Great North Road, is the *Ram Jam Inn*, formerly the *Winchelsea Arms*. Under the latter name, it was a haunt of Dick Turpin, the notorious highwayman, but sometime in the 'coaching days', according to local legend, a passenger was set down at the inn who immediately charmed everybody with his wit, stories and general behaviour. In a moment of generosity he promised the management that before he left he would impart the secret of how to draw mild and bitter from the same barrel. As the time of his departure drew near, he left his baggage at the door and, seeking the wife of the innkeeper, offered to divulge the promised knowledge. In the cellar he chose a barrel. 'Now' he said, 'we will make a hole on the left side so, and you ram your thumb against it. Having done that, we make a hole on the other side and you jam your other thumb against that.' Then, claiming to have forgotten the spilepegs, he told her to hold on tight while he ran upstairs and fetched them. He was never seen again and the innkeeper returned later to discover his wife still embracing the beer-barrel for dear life.

Over the entrance of the same inn a carved stone commemorates a prize-fight which took place nearby, at Thistleton Gap, between the famous pugilists Tom Cribb and the negro, Molyneux. It was the second time that the two had been matched to contest the championship and the fight was won by Cribb after twenty minutes. A small farm close by, known as Cribb's Lodge, still marks the site of the fight.

Cribb was champion of England from 1808-18 and his contests with Molyneux are considered by some to have been the first world championship fights. Cribb was born at Bitton (Glos) but there is no sign to him in that county, although a few years ago the *Union Arms*, Panton Street, London, was renamed the *Tom Cribb* in his memory.

An inn which was one of the original pilgrim hostels and is still thriving, is the famous *George* at Amesbury (Wilts). It was originally attached to Amesbury Abbey but became Crown property at the Dissolution. From records dated 1541, it is known that the house was formerly the *George & Dragon*. In the Civil War General Fairfax used the inn as his headquarters. It was also the halfway stop of the famous West Country 'Quicksilver Mail', mentioned elsewhere in these pages.

The real stuff of history is embodied in the *Eclipse*, Winchester (Hants), a fine half-timbered building which was once the rectory of nearby St Lawrence church. Formerly there was a *Sun Inn* on the opposite side of the road but the new inn stole the trade, hence the apt name. In 1685, Dame Alice Lisle, who had sheltered some poor wretches from Monmouth's defeated army at Sedgmoor, was tried at the Bloody Assizes and stepped from an upper window of the *Eclipse* to the scaffold where she was beheaded. She had the ill-fortune to be arrested by a colonel whose father had been sentenced to death by her husband some years before. The jury were reluctant to convict her at the trial, but Judge Jeffreys overruled their scruples and sentenced her to be burned alive. She petitioned James II, who granted her plea to be beheaded instead.

It must be rare indeed for an inn to be named as a reminder of archaeological history. An instance, however, is the *Anglo-Saxon*, Bidford-on-Avon (Warw) for it is adjacent to the site of an Anglo-Saxon burial ground that was excavated in 1922-3, when jewellery and some 170 skeleton remains were discovered.

A nice piece of legend-cum-fairy story surrounds the *Three Nuns*, Mirfield (W.R. Yorks). It adjoins the site of the ancient Kirklees Priory, where Robin Hood is said to have been buried and where he was tended at the last by the nuns. For good measure, Maid Marion is said to have ended her days in the same nunnery.

From the thirteenth century, there was an inn named the *Ship* at Restronguet Creek, nr Falmouth (Corn). About 1789 HMS 'Pandora' was sent to look for mutineers from HMS 'Bounty' and while returning with some of the fugitives ran on to a reef and foundered, a mishap which cost the captain his commission. He then bought the 'Ship' inn and renamed it the *Pandora* after his ship.

Foy Boat, Ramsgate (Kent), has a recently completed sign by the artist, Brian Thomas, depicting this particular type of craft which once served the sailing ships as they lay off the Kentish coast awaiting favourable winds. These small, fast vessels ferried supplies to the ships in a very lucrative trade which amounted to £50,000 or £60,000 a year. The original *Foy Boat* was 'blitzed' during the last war but the present new building carries on the name and the tradition.

At Blackburn (Lancs) the *Old Mother Redcap* perpetuates a name which has been handed down from Elizabethan times. The woman was a witch—a fierce one to judge from the fine sign—and it was said that her presence, in company with the Prince of Darkness, always foretold disaster. Legend also has it that her spell could only be broken if she were encircled with a golden ring—a feat finally accomplished by trapping her in an iron fetter which concealed a similar one of gold.

The *Bell*, Woodham Walter (Essex), has a sign with 'I greet the living—the dead I mourn' inscribed in Latin beneath the bell. Another portly person was associated with this place, one Edward Bright, who at the time of his death at the age of twenty-six weighed forty-five stone. The customers of the inn laid bets as to how many people could be buttoned up in his overcoat, which was found easily to accommodate seven persons.

At the *Rose & Crown*, Bainbridge (Yorks), a centuries-old custom is perpetuated when a horn is blown at 9 o'clock every night from the end of September to Shrove Tuesday. The hornblower, a local man, can maintain a top C note for seven seconds and under the right conditions can be heard over a distance of three miles. The origin of the custom was to guide travellers over the remote and wild countryside. The original buffalo horn used for the purpose now reposes in Bolton Castle museum. The one now in use was presented to the village in 1864.

Another interesting old custom still survives at *Ye Olde Globe*, Berrynarbor (N. Devon), where the ceremony of the ashen faggot has been carried on for centuries. Every Christmas Eve a bundle of ash wands, bound with strips of supple ash, is carried in with due ceremony and from the last of the old fire the new one is lit. Originally a pagan ceremony, the practice now commemorates the tradition that the newly-born Christ was warmed at a fire of ash wands, the only wood that will burn when green.

High up on the Greenhow moors between Pateley Bridge and Grassington (Yorks) there is still a *Miners' Arms*, for this area was once the centre of much mining activity. The Romans obtained lead from the mines here and in the nineteenth century ore was still being extracted on a large scale. Today there are abandoned underground workings in the vicinity, where scores of miles of tramway track still lie. Very often a *Miners' Arms* in a remote and un-expected part of the countryside gives a clue to former activities in the area. North Molton (Devon) has such a reminder of the great copper mines which were worked there in the early 1860s.

Almost 150 years ago a horse-drawn tramway was built between Plymouth and Princetown to carry supplies to the prison and bring back peat from the moors. It was in its way quite an engineering feat, for Princetown, at 1,400 ft above sea level, is the highest town in England. A notorious S-bend on the journey across the moor gave its name to the inn, the *Devil's Elbow*.

The *Blue Boar*, Cambridge, has in the entrance hall a magnificent carving of the animal, which was the badge of the de Veres, Earls of Oxford. The carving is believed to be over five centuries old and was originally the sign of the house which occupied the site of the present one in 1550. The first reference to an inn on the site was in 1693, when the churchwardens of All Saints, the venerable church up the road, spent 2s 'for beer at the *Blue Boar* on ye Queen's Birthday'. Later the inn became the coaching house for the Sheffield, Birmingham, Norwich and Ipswich route.

Help the Poor Struggler is an inn at Hollinwood, a suburb of Oldham (Lancs) and, appropriately enough this was kept from about 1948 to 1955 by Albert Pierrepoint, the public hangman. Locally it is recalled that, during his tenancy, a notice on display stated: 'No hanging around this bar'! Pierrepoint later moved to the *Rose & Crown*, Much Hoole (Lancs).

━━━━━━━━━━

Hero of Aliwal, Whittlesey, nr Peterborough (Northants), is a tribute to Sir Harry Smith (1787-1860), who was born at Whittlesey. A brilliant soldier, he served in America and took part in all the principal battles of the Peninsular War. He also fought in the Sikh campaign in India and distinguished himself by leading the charge against the Sikhs at Aliwal in 1846. In South Africa, towns named after him include Harrismith, Ladysmith (his wife) and Aliwal.

━━━━━━━━━━

Close to the entrance of Queensway (Mersey tunnel) between Birkenhead and Liverpool, is an inn called the *Free Library*, a name it received because of its proximity to the public library opened in 1864. The present library, a new one, is a mile away from the inn which shares its name.

━━━━━━━━━━

In the village of North Cadbury, nr Yeovil (Som), there is an inn with a name which takes us far back into history, for the *Catash* is named after the Hundred of Catsash, and the Court of Catsash was held beneath the ash trees on a site still known as Three Ashes. The middle 's' has been left out of the inn's name for obvious reasons.

━━━━━━━━━━

Very old is the *Royal Children*, Nottingham, so-named because Princess Anne, daughter of James II, used to play

Page 125: An up to date sign at Plymouth, close to where the great
yachtsman ended his voyage

Page 126: (*top left*) Folkestone (Kent); (*top right*) Sharpness; (*bottom*)
In contrast to the village inn, the *Mayflower* on the Thames is typical of
the scores that used to abound on the river

with the innkeeper's children. Over the door of this inn is a bone said to come from a whale, a sign which indicated that whale oil was sold there. The inn was one of the first to use lamps instead of candles.

Many travellers must have admired the splendid wrought-iron bracket which supports the sign of the *Ship*, Mere (Wilts). The ironwork, which terminates in a bunch of gilded grapes, was the work of a local clockmaker about the middle of the eighteenth century. The house was built by Sir John Coventry, who lived there until 1682. He became famous in the third quarter of the seventeenth century when, because of derogatory remarks about the king and Nell Gwyn, he was set upon by ruffians and his nose slit to the bone. There was a great outcry which resulted in the passing of a special Act of Parliament declaring such mutilation an act of felony and subject to the death penalty.

All sorts of artists and craftsmen have been responsible for producing inn signs, but unique is the sign of the *George*, Piercebridge (Co. Durham). It bears a likeness of King George III, carved in wood, and a small mouse also figures in the design. The mouse was the symbol of the Thompson workshops at Kilburn (Yorks) and though found on church furniture all over the world, it must be unique on an inn sign.

At Camborne (Corn) is *Tyacks*, which has been known to generations of Cornishmen. The word 'tyack' is Cornish for 'farmer'.

H

In many parts of the British Isles, including Peebles (Scotland) and Sheffield, there are inns named *Tontine*, which were built by funds raised by a 'Tontine'. This was originally an arrangement by which parents with children of similar age deposited a certain sum of money with stakeholders for each child. The monies so collected remained intact until there was a sole survivor who took the whole. 'Tontines' were named after Lorenzo Tonti, an Italian banker who was responsible for introducing the scheme to France in 1643, in order to finance buildings schemes. The Sheffield *Tontine* was built in 1785 by the system, when fifty subscribers put up £100 each. The inn was sold in 1850 for £7,720.

At the *Falcon* on the Scarborough-Whitby road (Yorks) the fire in the grate has been burning continuously for over 300 years.

Part way down the main street of Combe Martin (N. Devon), the longest village in England, stands a queer-shaped building. It is the *Pack of Cards*, which has been an inn since 1716. Originally built by an eccentric local squire, it has fifty-two windows, though prior to the window tax there were even more. The building has a compelling resemblance to a card castle such as a child might build. A rare piece of furniture is the press-gang table of refectory type that differs from the general style in that the top is 10 ft long by 4 ft wide and more than 12 in deep. If the alarm was given that the 'Press' were approaching, men liable to be taken could easily hide in it.

Ye Olde Albion, Crantock, nr Newquay (Corn), displays as its sign a picture of the 90-gun HMS 'Albion', launched at Plymouth in 1842. In fact, however, the inn is named after a schooner which was built in the Gannel shipyard a mile or so away. Crantock was once a thriving port and its 400-year old inn has a smuggler's hole beside the fireplace, where contraband used to be hidden. It is now blocked up for safety. Each fireplace at the inn has its individual pasty oven and until a few years ago the water supply was drawn from a deep well below the bar.

The fact that hotels, not only in this country but all over Europe, carry the name of *Bristol* is due to an extraordinary character who lived from 1730 to 1803. Born Frederick Hervey, he became Earl Bishop of Derry and on the death of his brother in 1779 succeeded to the Earldom of Bristol and a vast income. He was a great traveller and recognised as a connoisseur of good living wherever he went, so that the hotels in which he elected to stay became known as 'Lord Bristol's Hotel'—an assurance of the highest possible standards. A great patron of the arts, he erected a grandiose castle on the Londonderry coast in which to house his treasures. Downhill Castle is now a fantastic ruin, but his lordship's fame survives in the many great cities of Europe—Paris, Rome, Berlin, Vienna and others—where there is still a *Hotel Bristol*.

On a night in August 1965, the sign of the *New Inn*, Cradley (Herefs), mysteriously disappeared. A few days later a new sign depicting a horse in its stable, and obviously painted in haste, took its place. For some weeks the matter remained a mystery but eventually the artist was traced and a meeting arranged between him and the brewery company (Messrs Flowers). It transpired that the sign had been painted as a prank but, having been given so much publicity, it was felt that the new name should stay. So the same artist painted a permanent sign and the inn was re-named the *Stable*.

Though there is a wealth of history surrounding the old taverns which were once situated in and about the wynds and closes of Edinburgh's old town, little of the city's great traditions are reflected in the names of its inns. Perhaps the reason is that the taverns were mostly appalling places which did not lend themselves to being glamorised, the Scottish innkeeper of those days being primarily a stabler whose first attention was given to the traveller's horse.

One inn, the *Hole i'-th' Wall*, was so-called because there was a piece of the old Flodden wall nearby. There is a *Greyfriars Bobby*, with its beautiful story, and two inns —*Deacon Brodie's* tavern and *Deacon's Den*—which perpetuate the name of a notorious scoundrel. This was William Brodie, a town councillor and a deacon of the city, who flourished in the 1780s. A cabinet-maker by trade and apparently the acme of respectability, he nevertheless had the reputation of being very crafty. The full extent of his double life, however, was not apparent until he was apprehended for breaking into the General Excise office and stealing money. This led to proof of his complicity in many other large-scale thefts, including entering a bank by means of a false key and carrying off £800 in notes. After a long search he was eventually arrested in Amsterdam and brought back to stand trial before four judges. Both Brodie and his accomplice, a grocer named

George Smith, were found guilty and were hanged at the Tolbooth in 1778. A third man implicated was John Brown, who turned King's evidence at the trial. Crafty to the last, it is said that Brodie bribed the executioner to allow him to wear a steel collar to prevent strangulation.

Just across the river bridge by the remote and very ancient church of Hubberholme, near the village of Buckden (Yorks), is the building which formerly served as a rectory. About 100 years ago, however, the church authorities turned the house into an inn and named it *The George*, rehousing the vicar in three cottages close by which they converted for his use. The sign of the inn formerly illustrated the White Rose of York, the arms of the Bradford diocese and the Cross of St George. Here, on every New Year's Eve, a plot of land bequeathed for the benefit of the poor of the parish and known as the 'Poor Pasture', is put up for auction and 'knocked down' to the farmer making the highest bid for the next year's tenancy. The auction is always preceded by a special sermon for which the officiating clergyman is paid 6s. In 1965, the Church Commissioners sold the property, though it still remains an inn.

The village of East Harlsey, between Stokesley and Northallerton (Yorks), was way back in history a place of call for the raiders who came from over the Scottish border. Known as caterans or 'cats', they were no doubt accompanied by their fellows who played bagpipes; hence, so legend says, the inn became the *Cat & Bagpipes*, and still bears this name today.

A most unlikely name for an inn would seem to be the *Shoulder of Mutton & Cucumbers*, yet this name of the inn at Yapton, nr Arundel (Sussex), is perfectly justified. Two centuries ago cucumber sauce was a local delicacy always served with mutton and the dish became so famous and was so much appreciated by coach travellers that the inn adopted it as its name. At Shelf, nr Halifax (Yorks) there is a *Shoulder of Mutton*.

At Kingston, nr Lewes (Sussex), is an inn bearing a name which recalls that, in years past, there was a regular traffic of men carrying fish from Brighton to Lewes. Known as 'juggs', they used to stop at a cottage in Kingston for a rest. In time the cottage became an inn, and what more appropriate name than the *Jugg's Arms*?

Years ago the limestone cliffs at Stony Middleton (Derbys) formed a deep gorge and a young woman, after a lover's quarrel, jumped from them to end her life. She was saved by her billowing crinoline which acted as a parachute and the inn at the foot of the cliffs is now known as *Lover's Leap*.

An unusual dilemma faced the brewers when the sign of the *King's Head*, Shotley Bridge (Co. Durham), was due for repainting in 1960. No one was sure which monarch was reigning when the licence was first granted, so a compromise was reached and the signboard has the likeness of Henry VIII on one side and Charles I on the other. With a span of 100 years or so between them, honour is satisfied.

The sign of the *Marquis of Anglesea*, in London, W.C.2, portrays Henry William Paget, who was a very popular commander of cavalry at the battle of Waterloo, where he lost a leg. The story goes that, when close to the Duke of Wellington at the battle, a cannon ball severed his leg and he exclaimed to his chief : 'By God, I've lost my leg.' The Duke, glancing up from his maps, replied : 'By God, so you have', and returned his attention to the battle. The leg was buried in a garden close by, but was placed with the rest of Paget's remains when he died. After Waterloo, Paget was created Marquis of Anglesea in recognition of his services.

Nearly two hundred years ago, in 1783, there was a space race at Versailles, when Montgolfier, son of a paper manufacturer, made the first ascent in a hot-air balloon of his own invention, taking with him some animals. An inn sign at the *Air Balloon*, nr Brockworth (Glos), commemorates this event.

At Whitehaven (Cumb) the former *Wheatsheaf* has been renamed the *Paul Jones*, after the notorious and brilliant naval adventurer who had connections with Whitehaven. Born in 1747, he was apprenticed to a shipowner in the town and later served five years on a slaver before becoming a buccaneer. In the course of his extraordinary career he once returned to Whitehaven to raid the harbour. Later, he joined the American Navy, in which he became a commander, and fought the British. He then sailed under the French flag and finally became a rear-admiral in the Russian navy. He died in 1792, at the age of forty-five.

From time immemorial the Ypres Tower at Rye (Sussex) has been a look-out post. Marauders, from the Danes to the German planes of 1939-45, have been searched for and found from this vantage point. Appropriately, therefore, just below the tower is the *Ypres Castle*, now a popular inn for fishermen.

The *Drovers*, Fairseat (Kent), lost its rural name when a local man returned from the naval battles of the eighteenth century. He had fought with Admiral Rooke at the battle of Vigo in 1702, when the French and Spanish fleets were overwhelmed. On taking the inn, he promptly renamed it *Vigo* and as such it still flourishes.

Into the front of the *Running Pump*, Catforth (Lancs), is built a pump which bears the date 1834. Apparently the inn was once the centre to which villagers went to draw water and served the community for many years.

The *Ostrich* inn, Colnbrook (Bucks), which, 800 years ago, was a hospice attached to a monastery justifiably claims to be one of the oldest inns in the country. Always associated with it is the story of an unscrupulous landlord of the sixteenth century, named Jarman, who assigned his more wealthy clients to a special room where the bed rested on a hinged trap. When the guest was asleep, Jarman would release a catch causing the bed to tip its occupant into the cellar below, where he was promptly murdered and robbed.

The *Red Cow*, situated on the highest point of Canvey Island (Essex), was used as a base for the RAF rescue teams fighting the disastrous floods which ravaged the island a few years ago. When eventually the water subsided, the inn was appropriately renamed *King Canute*.

The legend of the Lambton worm, the subject of a north country dialect song, is kept alive by the *Lambton Worm*, an inn at Chester-le-Street (Co. Durham). The legend is about a monster worm caught in the river by the young Lord Lambton, who threw it down a well and then went off to fight in the Crusades. The worm, like the Loch Ness monster, grew to gargantuan proportions and terrorised the district, eating cattle and children. News was sent to the young lord, who then returned and cut the monster into two.

In 1965, a lorry driver left the *New Inn*, Ponts Hill, nr Ross-on-Wye (Herefs), for Birmingham and on arrival at his destination found a hen had travelled the whole way on the axle of his lorry. On the return journey, she was given a more comfortable trip in the cab. No ordinary hen, she insisted on paying for the ride by laying an egg *en route* and must have enjoyed her experience, for a little later she travelled again on the same axle to Cardiff. The inn was later re-named the *Travelling Hen* and the wandering bird, called 'Loosey', was a VIP at the opening ceremony.

On the North Yorkshire moors (the Pickering/Whitby road) is the *Saltersgate Inn*. The 'gate' is derived from the Saxon 'way' and, standing on the route from coastal to inland towns, recalls that there was once a considerable traffic in salt. A condition of tenure at the inn is that the peat fire, which has been burning continuously for 166 years, shall never be allowed to go out.

••••••••••••

Built in 1678, an inn in the small village of Shebbear (N. Devon) has in recent years had its name changed from the 'New Inn' to the *Devil's Stone*, to identify it with the legend associated with a huge stone which lies under a 600-year-old oak tree in front of the church across the road. On 5 November each year it is the villagers' custom to turn this stone over to the accompaniment of the church bells, for it is said to have been dropped by the Devil who may still be lurking there and could bring misfortune to the village unless driven out each year.

••••••••••••

The 'Boot' is a fairly common inn sign but the *Boot* at Liscard (Ches) has a special claim to fame. Legend has it that a highwayman was once captured because he fled the inn hurriedly, leaving one of his boots on a bed—and, to prove it, the boot is proudly preserved in a glass case in the lounge. There is also a *Boot & Shoe* in the small village of Greystoke (Cumb).

••••••••••••

The *Wheatsheaf*, Halifax (Yorks), was recently re-named the *William Dighton* to recall the public service of a former citizen of that name. A Customs & Excise officer in the city, he was primarily responsible for the eventual smashing of the Cragg Vale coining gang which flourished in the district in the eighteenth century.

Led by 'King' David Hartley and James Oldfield, the gang

specialised in clipping coins and making counterfeit money, and used the *Dusty Miller* at Mytholmroyd (Yorks) as their meeting place. Dighton's good detective work put him close on their trail and, fearing imminent arrest, the gang waylaid him near his home in Bull Close Lane, Halifax, and shot him through the head. The authorities promptly offered £100 reward for information which would lead to an arrest and a local attorney, Robert Parker, who had been working with Dighton, intensified his efforts to secure evidence. Just a year afterwards he was successful in bringing Hartley and Oldfield to justice. They were executed in 1770, but some forty others who had been arrested were set free for want of evidence. Another five years went by before Dighton's murderers were, in turn, brought to justice and executed. One of them, Robert Thomas, made a full confession but was nevertheless hanged at York in 1774.

The exploits of this gang were the basis of a novel: 'Back o' The Moon' by Oliver Onions and their coin-clipping activities were largely responsible for the subsequent introduction of pocket guinea-weighing machines to protect the public against coins which were being debased by as much as 20 per cent.

＊＊＊＊＊＊＊＊＊＊＊＊

Perhaps one of the most intriguing examples in recent years of a re-named inn is to be found at Windscales (Cumb) where the inn, which for years was the *Royal Oak*, is now called *Oily Johnnie's*. Many years ago the inn's licensee also 'peddled' paraffin oil around the district, and was known by the affectionate nickname of 'Oily Johnnie'. When the place was modernised, his name was a natural choice, accepted enthusiastically by the locals, and no doubt attracts a welcome 'curiosity' trade.

＊＊＊＊＊＊＊＊＊＊＊＊

The *Three Arrows*, Boroughbridge (Yorks), takes its name from the famous monoliths known as the Devil's Arrows, which are close by. It is believed that the stones came originally from Plompton, some fifteen miles away, are thought to date from the Bronze Age, and were probably connected with some pagan ritual. The largest of the 'arrows' is 30 ft high, including the 6 ft below the ground.

There is a fascinating history behind the name of the *King's Wark* on Leith Shore, nr Edinburgh, where records of the building go back to the first half of the fifteenth century. The King's Wark originally served as a military storehouse, and later as a residence which was used from time to time by royalty, including Mary Queen of Scots.

Almost totally destroyed in 1544, when the English forces invaded, the building was restored twenty years later, and used, among other purposes, as a reception centre for plague victims. The area was then bestowed upon one of the king's grooms-in-chamber, together with certain privileges, including a tax of £4 to be levied on every tun of wine sold in the taverns of the King's Wark, which were never to exceed four in number.

Today, only one of the buildings is still known as the *King's Wark*, and to seamen from the four corners of the world as 'The Jungle'. The place has low-ceilinged, beamed rooms and the panelled walls are three feet thick at the window embrasures. The original cellars, which the old records say were 'to be kept watertight to receive the King's wine and other provisions', are still in use.

The market towns of the Lake District have many ancient and famous inns. The *George*, Keswick (Cumb), was formerly the *George & Dragon* but on the accession of

George I, the second half of the name was dropped. There, in Elizabethan days, the queen's collector received the dues from the German miners who extracted lead and silver from the surrounding hills. Not all the ore which changed hands there was above suspicion, for much illicit trading was done at the inn, as is recounted by Walpole in 'Rogue Herries'. At the *George* also, the young Earl of Derwentwater stayed to drink ale before setting off to raise a troop at Caldbeck to support the Jacobite Rebellion of 1715. The Earl was later arrested and lodged in the Tower of London, and though Walpole is said to have been offered £60,000 for his release, he was beheaded on Tower Hill at the age of twenty-nine. On the night of his death the Aurora Borealis was particularly bright and in the Lake District this display in the heavens is still known as 'Lord Derwentwater's Lights'.

The *Oak & Ivy*, Hawkhurst (Kent), was once the headquarters of a desperate gang of smugglers known as the Hawkhurst gang, who operated in Sussex about the mid-eighteenth century. A well-organised group of escaped convicts under the leadership of Arthur Gray, the gang numbered up to 100, and whereas most smugglers were anxious to avoid encounters with Customs officers, the Hawkhurst men carried arms and were prepared to use them. Dissension within the gang once led to a number of them being caught and imprisoned at Newgate, but they managed to escape and the gang were later involved in a fight with revenue officers who interrupted a raid on a Customs house. An informer among them was subsequently murdered, together with a Customs officer, and the gang was finally broken up in 1749, when a number of the men were arrested and hanged.

In the Washburn Valley, off the Harrogate/Skipton road (Yorks), the village of West End was served by the *Gate* inn. A few years ago the inn closed its door forever when the village was evacuated and flooded to form part of the 1,727 million gallons capacity Thruscross reservoir, to augment the water supply for Leeds.

●●●●●●●●●●●

The discovery of an old print in the local council offices reminded the Workington Brewery Company of the former importance of Maryport (Cumb) as a port. It showed Irish cattle being 'landed' by the unceremonious method of 200 years ago of pushing them overboard and making them swim for it. The print was copied and as a mural now adorns the *Fo'c'sle* (formerly the *Globe*) in Maryport.

Some Modern Signs

IF the naming of inns continues to follow the trend of the last two to three hundred years in remembering great men held in high esteem, we are likely to see many more signs in the years to come bearing the likeness of Sir Winston Churchill. What appears to have been the first of them adorns a new inn opened on the outskirts of Rochdale (Lancs) in August 1965, and Lady Churchill sent one of her favourite photographs of the great man, so that the artist could copy it for the signboard. Painted in oils, it shows Sir Winston as he was about fifty years ago, wearing one of his favourite blue and white spotted bow-ties, and attracts much attention.

Another striking feature of the building is a mural in the

entrance hall measuring 9 ft by 7 ft 3 in and depicting Sir Winston in some of the varied roles of his eventful life— soldier, sailor, pilot, writer and politician. Scores of photographs were sifted through before the final choice was left to the artists responsible for the mural.

On the walls of one of the public rooms—the Marlborough lounge—there is a display of the late Sir David Low's famous wartime cartoons of Churchill and the inn itself, appropriately enough, is situated in War Office Road.

Also in 1965, another *Winston Churchill* was opened at Dunstable (Beds).

Yet another, with a sign showing the great man giving his famous war-time V sign, is the *Churchill* in the village of that name in Somerset.

For centuries the old *Crown & Anchor*, Plymouth, looked out over the cobbled streets to the quayside, once the scene of great events in English history and now the busy base of a modern fishing fleet. Less than a mile away, in August 1966, Francis Chichester set off in his 'Gipsy Moth IV' to sail round the world alone. It was fitting, therefore, that when the *Crown & Anchor* became due for rebuilding, Messrs Starkey, Knight & Ford, the brewers, should seek permission to call it the *Sir Francis Chichester* and so it was re-named in December 1967 in the presence of the Lord Mayor of Plymouth, the opening ceremony being performed by the great yachtsman himself.

The house has a single bar, the décor of which features several mementoes of his world voyage, as well as photographs relating to his early exploits. Chichester emigrated to New Zealand in 1919 at the age of eighteen, and eight years later had made £10,000. He learned to fly, returned to England and in 1929 became the second man to fly solo from England to Australia, and subsequently the first man to fly alone over the treacherous Tasman Sea from New Zealand to Australia. Most of the exhibits, however, relate to his circumnavigation of the world and include: an extensive collection of photographs covering his voyage from Plymouth in 1966 up to the bestowal of the accolade at Greenwich on 7 July 1967; photostat copies of his log entries; a 3-ft model of 'Gipsy Moth IV'; two prints of paintings of 'Gipsy Moth IV' off Cape Horn, one by Montague Dawson entitled 'Horn a' Beam', the original of which was presented by Colonel W. H. Whitbread to Sir Francis on his safe return to England; the famous 'Chichester yachting cap' which he wore during the voyage and, of course, the specially designed 4½-gallon container of Whitbread Tankard ale which Sir Francis carried on 'Gipsy Moth IV'.

The inn sign, designed and painted by John Cook of West Country Breweries, shows Sir Francis in his famous cap looking out towards 'Gipsy Moth IV' riding at anchor in the harbour, while in the foreground a globe of the world traces his route.

Sir Francis Chichester's yacht is also honoured by another Plymouth inn. The house, situated on Citadel Road, changed its name to *Gipsy Moth IV* when the lone voyager landed after his feat.

Even more up-to-date is the new establishment at Bracklesham (Sussex) opened in 1968 and named the *Lively*

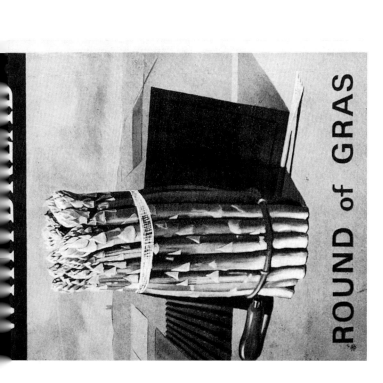

Page 143: Two unusual modern signs: (*left*) 'The Round of Gras' at Badsey (Worcs); (*right*) 'The Frogmill' at Shipton Oliffe (Glos)

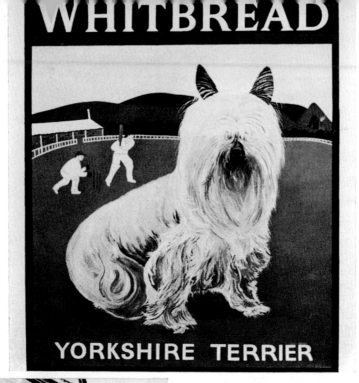

Page 144: (top) An appealing sign at Brinsworth (Yorks) (bottom left) A new conception of a former religious sign at Stokesley (N.R. Yorks); (bottom right) A splendid historical sign nr. Tewkesbury

Lady after Sir Alec Rose's yacht, which he had sailed single-handed round the world a few months previously.

•••••••••••

Yet another new sign in Plymouth is that of *The Walrus*, commemorating a famous amphibian aircraft of the 1930s, built by the Supermarine Company and extensively used in air-sea rescue operations.

•••••••••••

Among the modern inns that have risen from the ruins of bombed London is the *Magpie & Stump*, Old Bailey. It stands on the site of a Pickwickian establishment, from whose upstairs rooms it was said that diners in days gone by were able to enjoy a close-up view of the public hangings. Much frequented by Whigs in its earlier days, it is now popular with members of the Press and others engaged in Old Bailey cases.

•••••••••••

By no means the least pleasing of modern signs are those which identify a local man and one such is *John Brunt*, Paddock Wood (Kent). Brunt won the Victoria Cross in Italy in 1944, when serving with the Sherwood Foresters, only to die the following day.

•••••••••••

Similarly the *Jolly Sailor*, West Bromwich (Staffs) carries on its sign the portrait of a local brewery worker who lost his life serving on convoy duty. After the war the brewers had the happy idea of re-naming an inn in his memory.

•••••••••••

I

The *Flying Saucer*, Gillingham (Kent), has a two-sided sign. One shows the popular conception of a flying saucer in orbit, while the reverse shows a giant saucer slipping from a woman's hand and heading directly for her startled spouse.

Dock Green, Leeds (Yorks), was officially opened in 1965 by Jack Warner, the actor, who plays the title role in the ever-popular television series 'Dixon of Dock Green'. The inn is on the site of what was previously Harehills Police Station.

It was odd that the great man responsible for rebuilding so much of London after the Fire of 1666 had never been honoured by an inn sign, and this has now been rectified by the new house *Sir Christopher Wren*, in Cathedral Close, adjoining his greatest work, St Paul's Cathedral. Nearby is another new house, the *Master Gunner*.

Brewery companies have been quick to name new houses in association with space travel. There is a *Man in Space*, nr Stoke-on-Trent (Staffs), a *Spotted Cow*, Betchworth (Surrey), which has a humorous sign on the same subject, and *The Other Side of the Moon*, Nottingham, which features 'Lunar III's' canine passengers.

At Taunton (Som) the sign of the *Full Moon* shows some Martian figures standing on a spaceship watching other rockets in orbit.

Broad Highway, Woodlands, Doncaster (Yorks), and *Flyover*, Yeadon (W.R. Yorks), represent the new road systems and the sign of the *Hand-in-Hand*, Tadworth (Surrey), shows children using a zebra crossing.

After more than 100 years in business the *New Inn*, Greasby (Cheshire), was recently demolished and a new building erected named *The Red Cat*. The name refers to a sandstone corbel, probably meant to be a lion's head, in nearby St Hugh's chapel, built in 1398. The decorative theme in the bars of the new house is that of the mythical cats of witches and millers of medieval England.

An interesting feature of the rear lounge, known as the 'Mill' room, is a pair of working mill wheels. The centre of the backfitting is taken up with the main drive wheel, which is 8 ft in diameter and face-cogged. This drives the centre wheel on the ceiling which is cogged to the 5-ft outer wheels. Both wheels are made of timber to the pattern of the old 'peg' mills—which were timber mills of light construction with a centre post embedded in the ground. The miller was able to bring the sails of the mill into the wind by turning the whole structure round. It is of interest to note that the original Bidston Mill which stood nearby was a peg mill, and the marks of the peg in block can still be seen and followed through 360° circumference of the centre post.

The front of the bar counter consists of oak-staved and brass-banded barrels, and the top is of copper, which reflects the movements of the wheels and the oak beamed ceiling of the servery area. The 'Mill' room's main ceiling area is of adzed beams with a trimmed centre section, in the manner of a loading bay for sacks, which is illuminated on all faces and acts as the main lighting source for the room.

One of the largest 'inn signs' in the country must be that famous locomotive, the 'Hayling Billy', which stands in the forecourt of the *Hayling Billy*, Elm Grove, Hayling Island (Hants). Thousands of holidaymakers will remember with nostalgia the trips that were run by the engine from Havant to Hayling Island before the line was closed. A railway atmosphere has been created in the new house by fittings from old coaches, complete down to the handles, straps, racks, communication cords, etc.

A new inn at Smallthorne, Stoke-on-Trent (Staffs), is the first British Esperanto inn. It is called the *Green Star* (La Verdo Stelo) and the symbol of the Esperantists appears on its sign. A language guide hangs on the wall of the inn to assist customers who are not Esperantists.

After forty-three years as head horseman with the brewers, Young & Company, Charlie Butler has achieved lasting fame, for an inn at Mortlake, London, has been named after him.

One of the new inns of Messrs Everard's brewery is the *Tom Thumb*, Blaby (Leics), the only one of the name in existence. Tom Thumb was the pigmy hero of an ancient nursery tale and a famous nineteenth-century American dwarf, named Stratton, was known as General Tom Thumb.

The *Basset Hound* is a new inn of Messrs Threlfalls situated between Birkenhead and Heswall. The name derives initially from a thirteenth-century lord of the manor of Thingwall, Sir Ralph Basset, who fought beside Simon de Montfort at the battle of Evesham in 1265. Tribute to the basset hound's long tradition of hunting is paid in the names of the lounges—the 'Kennel' and the 'Doghouse'— which are decorated with horse brasses, post and hunting horns, etc.

Another new house built by the same company is the *Lighthouse* in Wallasey village (Cheshire). There was an inn of this name in 1810, which is thought to have been called after the new Brighton Lighthouse (Porch Rock) which was erected in 1827 as a shore light in the shipping approach to Liverpool. The theme of the new inn is the history of Wallasey and its connection with shipping. The 'Red Noses' bar is so-named after the rock formation on the shore which contained coves believed to run from the shore to the infamous *Mother Redcap*, a haunt of smugglers and wreckers.

And Still They Come

IT would take a very large volume to list all the odd names which have been given to inns for they are as numerous as the variety of their subjects.

Playing cards obviously lend themselves to colourful signs and it is strange there are not more of them. Particularly attractive are *Four-in-Hand*, Newcastle; *King's Head*, Bradford and *Eight Kings*, Portland (Dorset).

Lists of some of the more popular subjects have already

been given and here, to conclude, is a selection at random of names which would be difficult to classify :

 Bunch of Carrots, Hampton Bishop (nr Hereford)
 Broad Face, Abingdon (Berks)
 French Horn, Ware (Herts)
 Glue Pot, Harrogate (Yorks)
 Flowing Well, Sunningwell (Berks)
 Noughts & Crosses, Polperro (Cornwall)
 Brick Wall, Skipton (Yorks)
 Hand & Flower, Barnet (Herts)
 Hand & Heart, Hindley (Lancs)
 Fool's Nook, Sutton (Cheshire)
 Candlestick, nr Hatfield (Herts)
 Auld Lang Syne, Oldham (Lancs)

Even astrology has its quota of inn signs, which include *Star in the East*, London, S.E.10, *Plough*, London, S.W.4, *North Pole*, London, S.W.4; Luton (Beds) has a *Half Moon* and Barnsley (Yorks) a *Morning Star*. There are also *Three Stars*, a *Shooting Star*, Boreham Wood (Herts), and a *Ye Olde Sun*, St Neots (Hunts). *Seven Stars* has already been mentioned as a popular sign of religious origin, and there is a *North Star*, Steventon (Berks), a *Blue Moon*, Leeds (Yorks), a *Rising Moon* and a *Full Moon*. There are a number of inns called the *Plough* and a Whitbread sign at one of them features this constellation.

Finally, at Atherton (Lancs) there is the charmingly-named *Mountain Dew*. Who would not want to drink at the *Mountain Dew* inn?

Acknowledgements

FORTUNATELY, the importance of the sign is now being appreciated by more and more brewery companies, though in the North Country particularly there are still many fascinating names unillustrated by any sign. The Workington Brewery Company recently inaugurated a scheme whereby prosaic names such as 'Commercial' and 'Railway' are being replaced with new ones, wherever possible with local associations. Messrs Whitbreads and their associated companies have particularly effective sign departments, and many of the smaller companies are also showing commendable enterprise in this direction.

Grateful thanks are offered to the brewery companies and individual licencees who so readily co-operated and assisted me with information and sometimes photographs. Libraries, too, rarely failed to unravel knots which had defeated all others. I am also deeply indebted to all those who, having read my previous efforts, write to give me additional information, lists of inns in the area or to send me pictures. I always look forward to hearing from fellow enthusiasts of the subject and the day starts well for me when the post brings a new name or an odd story concerning inns.

Special thanks are due to the following who have been so helpful in supplying information and pictures:

Bass Charrington Group Ltd	Ind Coope Ltd
Courage (Eastern) Ltd	Morland & Co Ltd
Dutton's Blackburn Brewery Ltd	Robinson, Frederick, Ltd
Everards Brewery Ltd	Starkey, Knight & Ford
Flowers & Sons Ltd	Tamplin's Brewery Ltd
Higsons Brewery Ltd	Threlfalls (Liverpool & Birkenhead) Ltd

Tollemache & Cobbold Breweries Ltd
Truman Hanbury Buxton & Co Ltd
Trust Houses Ltd
Young & Co

Wadworth & Co Ltd
West Country Breweries Ltd
Whitbread & Co Ltd
Workington Brewery Company Ltd

General Index

Names of Inns appear under separate Index

Index of Inns

Almost all the names in the following list are followed by 'A R M S', 'T A V E R N' or something similar. For convenience and quick reference unless there is a special reason only the title is mentioned here. Italic figures refer to illustrations.

Bull in Spectacles, Lichfield
  (Staffs), 66
Bull in the Oak, 50, 66
Bull in th' Thorn, 66
Bullers Arms, 39
Bullfinch, 63
Bullfinch, Bussard Spreyton 76
Bullfinch (Lincs), 76
Bull's Head, 13
Bunch of Carrots, Hampton
  Bishop, nr Hereford, 150
Bunch of Cherries, 84
Bunch of Grapes, 61, 84
Burns, 88
Bush, 52
Bustard, 63
Bustard (Lincs), 63
Butchers Arms, Farnborough,
  (Hants) 114
Byron, 88

Cabbage, Sefton, Liverpool,
  (Lancs), 61
Cadland, The, Old Village,
  Chilwell (Notts), 86
Camel's Head, Devonport,
  (Devon), 63, 66
Candlestick, nr Hatfield (Herts),
  150
Cannon, 92
Canopus, Rochester (Kent),
  28
Canute, 31
Cape of Good Hope, Goole
  (Yorks), 93
Captain Cook, 48
Captain Webb, Wellington
  (Salop), 47
Carders, Atherton (Lancs), 59
Cardinal Wolsey, 48
Caribou, 63
Carnarvon Castle, Oxton,
  Birkenhead (Cheshire), 103
Carrion Crow, Oldham (Lancs),
  77
Carters Rest, 23
Case is Altered, Harrow
  (Middx), 50
Case is Altered, Woodbridge
  (Suffolk), 49
Castle, Ruthin (Denbigh), *71*
Cat & Bagpipes, East Harlsey
  (Yorks), 131

Cat & Cracker, Grain (Kent),
  102
Cat & Custard Pot, 63
Cat & Custard Pot, Shipton
  Moyne (Wilts), 66, *90*, 91
Cat & Fiddle, 56, 63, 66
Cat & Fiddle, Buxton
  (Derbys), 105
Cat & Fiddle, New Forest
  (Hants), 56
Cat & Fiddle, Sowton (Devon),
  56
Cat & Lion, 62
Cat & Lion, Stretton (Cumb),
  72
Cat & Mustard Pot, 66
Cat i' t' Wall, Halifax (Yorks),
  66
Cat i' the Window, 66
Catash, North Cadbury, nr
  Yeovil (Som), 124
Catherine Wheel, 52
Cavalier, Grindon (Staffs), *71*,
  93
C.B., in Richmond (Yorks),
  109
Chain & Gate, 22
Chained Bull, 66
Champion, The, Well St, Lon-
  don, 86
Charles Cotton (Derbys), 39
Charles XII, Heslington (ER
  Yorks), 85
Chase, 86
Cheddar Cheese, London, 62
Cheddar Cheese, Reading
  (Berks), 62
Chequers, 11, 56
Chequers, Chipping Norton
  (Oxon), 57
Chequers, Tonbridge (Kent),
  104
Cherry, 83
Cheshire Lines, Southport
  (Lancs), 27
Chestnut, 83
Chicken, 76
Chieftain Morecambe (Lancs),
  103
Childe of Hale, Hale (Lancs),
  116
Children's Inn, The, Hollins
  Moor (Cheshire), 112

K

Dog & Bacon, 67
Dog & Crook, 67
Dog & Duck, 67
Dog & Fox, 67
Dog & Gun, 67
Dog & Hedgehog, Huckley (Leics), 67
Dog & Pheasant, 67
Dog & Pot, Stoke Green (Bucks), 67
Dog & Snipe, 67
Dog House, Frilford (Berks), 67
Dolphin, 81, 93
Donkey & Bacon, 68
Double Barrel, Cheltenham (Glos), 62
Double Gloucester, Gloucester, 62
Dove, 77
Dover Patrol, Blackheath, London, 93
Downham Tavern, Bromley (Kent), 106
Dragon, 30, 68
Dragon's Head, 68
Dressers, Heywood (Lancs), 59
Drop Inn, Guiseley (Yorks), 98
Drover's, Fairseat (Kent), 134
Dr Syntax, Oldham (Lancs), 88
Drug Store, Chelsea, London, 113
Drum & Monkey, Brownlow (Salop), 74
Drummer, 92
Drunken Duck, Hawkshead (Lancs), 77
Duck, 77
Duchess of Sutherland, Holloway, London, 46
Duke of Brunswick, 39
Duke of Cambridge, 34
Duke of Clarence, 34
Duke of Cumberland, 40
Duke of Edinburgh, 34
Duke of Kent, 34
Duke of Leeds, Leedstown (Cornwall), 37
Duke of Marlborough, 43
Duke of York, 34
Duke William, 40
Dumb Flea, Meldreth (Cambs), 83

Dun Horse, Kendal (Westm), 70
Durham Ox, 74
Dusty Miller, Mytholmroyd (Yorks), 137
Dutch Birds, Oldham (Lancs), 77
Dyers, Littleborough (Lancs), 59

Eagle, 77
Eagle & Child, 57, 78
Eagle & Hind, Chelmsford (Essex), 78
Eagle Tavern, City Rd, London, 99, 100
Eaglet, 78
Earl Beatty, Motspur Park, London, 39
Earl Canning, Hartpury (Glos), 39
Earl Grey, 48
Earl Haig, Hertford (Herts), 41
Earl Haig, Hounslow (Middx), 41
Earl Russell, Bristol, 45, 48
Eclipse, Winchester (Hants), 120
Edward II, Merriott (Som), 31
Eight Bells, Chipping Campden (Glos), 55
Eight Kings, Portland (Dorset), 149
Elephant, 63, 68
Elephant & Castle, 56, 68
Elephant & Castle, London, 56
Elephant & Hind, Dover (Kent), 68, 97
Elephant's Head, Clapton, London, 68
Elephant's Nest, Tavistock (Devon), 68
Elm, 83
Empress of Russia, Finsbury, London, 37
Endymion, 88
English Rose, Bristol, 84
Engine & Tender, St Neots (Hunts), 27
Ensign Ewart, Edinburgh (Scotland), 93
Essex Serpent, 83
Ewe & Lamb, 68